I
HATE
OHIO STATE

RICH THOMASELLI

TRIUMPH
B O O K S

CONTENTS

INTRODUCTION

OH, HOW I HATE OHIO STATE

WHEN I SAT DOWN TO WRITE THIS BOOK, I knew that one of my old newspaper bosses, Steve Greenberg, who had recommended me to the publishers, was writing his own version of this book—*I Love Ohio State/I Hate Michigan*. (Of course, this is *not* a book I endorse nor encourage you to purchase. If former OSU coach Woody Hayes wouldn't pull over with his car on the verge of running out of gas to fill up in the state of Michigan, I strongly suggest you take a pass on anything that would even remotely line the pockets of an avowed Ohio State fan such as Mr. Greenberg. Why, if it were me, and this is just me talking now, I would buy *two* of this book before purchasing its counterpart.)

Now, taking on a book project is an endeavor not for the faint of heart. It takes time to research and then write 60,000 words—and God bless friends and fellow writers, like my *Detroit Free Press* buddy Michael Rosenberg, whose brilliant book on Bo Schembechler and Woody Hayes, *War As They Knew It*, was almost double that.

So Steve and I shared some research and some thoughts during the writing process, such as what we determined were the best and worst games of the Michigan–Ohio State rivalry, that sort of thing. I was reluctant, of course; why help an Ohio State guy, right? But, in the end, I had to look at it from the Christian point of view. WWBD—What Would Bo Do? Would Bo Schembechler turn his back on the grammar-, spelling-, and punctuation-challenged OSU grads/fans? Would Bo sit back and let them continue to write sentences such as, "Michigan has had there work cut out for them against Ohio State the last seven years?" Or would Bo do the right thing and say, "Hey, dumb-ass Buckeye! First of all, it's 'their,' not 'there,' and, second of all, it would be, 'Michigan has *its* work cut out.'"

So I was forced to spend way too much of my own time correcting basic fourth- and fifth-grade writing mistakes that Ohio State grads continue to make into their thirties, forties, and fifties, which left me with little energy to write the second introduction to this book that leads off the Ohio State portion.

Until I saw Steve's introduction in his book.

He decided to use a quote from Hayes to lead off his lesser, poorly received book, a quote that he felt probably captured the essence of Michigan–Ohio State.

> *You're going to Michigan? Why you dumb, no-good sonofabitch! You go right ahead. You go there, and when you play against Ohio State, we'll just see whether you gain a yard against us all day. We'll break you in two.*
>
> —Woody Hayes
> (having lost a recruit to that school up north)

At first, I laughed. Heartily. A grown man acting like a complete tool. What was this, grade school? The truly laughable part was that Hayes probably never realized that half the players he recruited in Ohio went to Michigan to escape him, and the other half went to Ohio State by default because they couldn't get in to Michigan.

Yet the more I thought about it, the quote actually *was* perfect...for this book.

Because nothing symbolizes the sham that is the Ohio State football program more than the two coaches who have led the most successful eras in its history—Woody Hayes and Jim Tressel. Hayes, the insane, crazed old man who constantly acted like the child-bully on the playground (see the quote above) and went out in a blaze of ignominy by slugging a player from another team on national television. And, um, yes Ohio State fans: while the small pocket of you choose to remember Woody Hayes as some sort of great coach, 99 percent of the rest of college football remembers him for what he really was and for suffering a meltdown because a player on another team intercepted a pass. Waaaah!! He took my ball! I'm gonna beat him up now! Waaaah!!

And then there's Tressel.

Remember the old Sam Kinison bit where he sits down at the piano, claiming he wrote a love song for his ex, but instead ends up ranting, "You used me! I want my records back!"

That's how Michigan fans feel right now.

You used us, Ohio State. You used us, Jim Tressel. Yup, you played us. You *cheated* us. We want our championship back. Yes, our 2006 national championship. Maybe we get blown out by Florida, as you did, in the title game. Maybe we don't. But the opportunity to have played for it was cheated from us.

By you.

Jim Tressel resigned as the Ohio State football coach during the writing of this book, on Memorial Day of 2011, in fact, after a series of transgressions by the coach which you can document in the timeline listed at the end of this introduction. In a nutshell, star quarterback Terrelle Pryor—a Michigan recruit—and several other players were caught up in the investigation of a Columbus tattoo parlor owner who was being investigated by the feds. Turns out the players traded signed memorabilia for discounted or free tattoos, and according to a former player at OSU, Ray Small, it wasn't the first time. The incidents came to light in December 2010, but the five players were allowed to play in the Sugar Bowl against Arkansas and were suspended for the first five games of the 2011 season.

Story over, yes?

Not so fast, my friends.

The problem here is that while everybody else in the world, OSU officials included, found out about this in December 2010, Tressel knew eight months earlier when he was tipped off in an email from a former Buckeye who is now an attorney. But Tressel failed to inform his superiors, or the NCAA, and went on his merry way, playing players who likely would have been ineligible for at least part of the 2010 season had he gone public with the story when he first found out.

Tressel signed an NCAA compliance form in September, saying he had no knowledge of any wrongdoing by athletes. His contract, in addition to NCAA rules, specified that he had to tell his superiors or compliance department about any potential NCAA rules violations.

Ohio State called a news conference on March 8, 2011, in which it handed Tressel a two-game suspension—which Tressel magnanimously (sarcasm intended) raised by self-imposing a five-game suspension to match that of his players—and fined him $250,000.

OSU athletics director Gene Smith and school president E. Gordon Gee both publicly backed Tressel, with Gee even going as far as to say, when asked if he had considered firing the coach, "No, are you kidding? Let me just be very clear: I'm just hopeful the coach doesn't dismiss me."

Three months later, Gee had no choice but to give Tressel the option to resign or be fired.

Which brings us back to 2006. Jim Tressel lied and cheated. Ohio State lied and cheated. If he did it in 2010, what's to make us think that he didn't do it in 2006, or any other year for that matter? And with yet another star quarterback in Troy Smith, the eventual Heisman Trophy winner, at the helm. Smith had been suspended for the 2004 Alamo Bowl and the 2005 season opener after it was determined he accepted $500 from a booster.

Quarterback Terrelle Pryor and his tattoo arrive at the Woody Hayes Complex in May 2011. Pryor, the highest profile recruit of Jim Tressel's now defunct 25-year career, is one of five Buckeyes who were suspended for the first five games of the 2011 season for taking money and tattoos from a local tattoo-parlor owner in exchange for team merchandise.

Just $500? Riiiiiiiight. Pull this other leg, and it plays "Jingle Bells."

The first reaction from Ohio State fans to Michigan fans will be, "Don't be holier than thou." The problem with that, of course, is thou art so easy to be holier than.

And it's not sour grapes, either. In 2010 Ohio State used players who shouldn't have been playing. There's no disputing that. So there's no reason to believe that wasn't the case in any other season under Jim Tressel.

Listen, no program is squeaky clean. The NCAA rules and regulations manual is, literally, the size of a phonebook. And since many people prefer to find phone numbers online these days and eschew—or perhaps haven't even seen—a phonebook, trust us when we say it's big. Michigan football had its issues with the NCAA in 2009–2010, when the university acknowledged it broke the rules when it came to practices. U-M admitted it exceeded NCAA limits on practice time and staff size, that it failed to properly monitor its football program, and that former graduate assistant coach Alex Herron lied to NCAA investigators.

That was a one-time infraction and, let's be blunt here. In the grand scheme of things, to paraphrase the immortal words of Allen Iverson, "We in here talkin' about practice. Listen. We talkin' about practice."

But this wasn't a one-time transgression by Tressel. He had NCAA issues while he was at Youngstown State. He had NCAA issues in the early 2000s with star running back Maurice Clarett. He had NCAA issues with Smith, and NCAA issues with Pryor. There is a pattern of abuse here, and he and OSU finally got caught with their hand in the cookie jar.

There is no valid reason to believe that this was a singular mistake. There's every valid reason to believe there has been a pattern of corruption during the Tressel era, 2006 included.

So why are we so hung up on 2006? Because as Michigan fans we walked away from that regular season with disappointment but a grudging respect. The Wolverines lost a No. 1–versus–No. 2 showdown with Ohio State 42–39 at Columbus, when both teams were undefeated and the winner of The Game was headed to the national championship contest. It was a great game, with no incidents, no problems. It was hard-fought on enemy territory, and came just a day after the legendary Bo Schembechler died.

Now, after the fact, we walk away with a far worse feeling.

Michigan was cheated out of an entire season. You know, sort of how the referees cheated Miami out of the 2002 national championship won by OSU on that bogus pass interference call in overtime.

Only worse.

The Wolverines, under then-coach Lloyd Carr, were gunning for their second national championship in nine years. They beat Vanderbilt and Eastern Michigan to open the season, whipped a vastly overrated No. 2 Notre Dame team on the road, navigated a difficult opening to the Big Ten season with wins over Wisconsin, at Minnesota, Michigan State, and at Penn State. Then U-M cruised past Iowa, Northwestern, Ball State, and Indiana to make it 11–0 and set up the showdown at No. 1 Ohio State.

STATS WE HATE

- Ohio State has won seven consecutive games versus Michigan prior to the beginning of the 2011 season, and nine of the last 10.

- Ohio State running back Archie Griffin remains the only two-time winner of the Heisman Trophy.

- The Buckeyes have had 130 All-Americans heading into the 2011 season, to Michigan's 126.

- Ohio State 31, Miami 24, double overtime, 2003 national championship

- 66–12–1—Ohio State's all-time record when ranked No. 1 in the country

OHIO STATE

Michigan opened the game by driving down the field and scoring on a Mike Hart touchdown run, the first of three that day for Hart, to take a 7–0 lead. OSU then came roaring back when Smith—the Troy Smith who was suspended by the NCAA the previous year—led a 14-play, all-pass drive to tie the score. It came on a one-yard touchdown pass to Roy Hall. The TD pass to Hall tied the game. Running back Chris "Beanie" Wells then broke off a 52-yard scoring run, Ted Ginn Jr. caught a 39-yard TD pass from Smith, and Anthony Gonzalez also caught a scoring pass from Smith, and the Buckeyes led 28–14 at the half.

In the second half, U-M pulled within 28–24 and 35–31 before OSU scored its final TD on a 13-yard pass from Smith to Brian Robiskie. The Wolverines scored a late TD and a two-point conversion to make it 42–39 with three minutes to play, but U-M could not recover the onside kick, and Ohio State ran out the clock.

But, do you see what we're driving at here? Troy Smith. Who knows who else? And you wonder why the first reaction to Jim Tressel's resignation and the knowledge of how Ohio State operates its corrupt program is bitterness.

Here's a brilliant take on the situation by the Michigan blog Genuinely Sarcastic.

> Nothing Ohio State has accomplished in the last 10 years is valid anymore. From Clarett, to Smith, to Pryor, and all the others in between, with the cars and the cash and the discounts and the cutting of corners, Ohio State is essentially an SEC school operating in the Midwest. Tressel is a proven, documented cheater, and if the NCAA has any balls at all, they will slap him with a show-cause order, blackballing him from ever coaching again.... Tressel entered into a perfect marriage with Ohio State back in the winter of 2001. A native son with enormous success at a lower level, but more than ready to take the next step. And a school so desperate to reverse their fortunes in that final game in late November, so eager to erase the sour taste of 2–10–1 from their mouths, willing to sell their souls at all costs if it means claiming dominance over "That School Up North." That is the culture of Ohio State football. The means don't matter whatsoever. As long as the end is a victory over Michigan, they will tolerate anything that comes their way. And now they deserve the darkest of fates.

The funny thing is, Michigan fans don't necessarily want Jim Tressel gone. Remember, this was the man who came in with the boastful speech when he was hired that OSU fans would be proud of their players in the classroom, in the community, and "especially in 310 days in Ann Arbor, Michigan, on the football field."

Surely, we all hope that Michigan ends its seven-year losing streak to the Buckeyes in November 2011. Yet, it will seem almost bittersweet. It will be like Patton's Eighth Army beating Germany's Seventh Panzer Division without Erwin "the Desert Fox" Rommel in charge. Ironically, when that game is played, it will be the first time in 82 years that both schools will have first-year head coaches on the sidelines for The Game— Michigan's Brady Hoke versus Ohio State's Luke Fickell.

It's the dawn of a new era.

But if it means an era without Ohio State being unethical, deceitful, and dishonorable, without the lying and corruption that Tressel brought, and, literally, without cheating another program out of what could have—should have?—been a victory, so be it.

And therein lies the difference between the University of Michigan and the Ohio State University. Integrity. Let me throw some names at you. Rex Kern. Archie Griffin. Eddie George. Vic Janowicz. Hopalong Cassady. Pete Stinchcomb. All great players, all great men. Who remembers, though, in the wake of Clarett, punks like David Boston, Tressel's blatant lies, and Tattoo Gate?

Those rings and baubles mean something to Michigan Men. To Ohio State players, they are merely trinkets to be sold or traded.

That alone should tell you the difference between Wolverines and Buckeyes.

OHIO STATE

JIM TRESSEL TIMELINE

(by Cleveland.com)

2001—Tressel is hired at OSU.

2003—OSU finishes its perfect 14–0 national season with a 31–24 double overtime victory against No. 1 Miami. It is Ohio State's first national title since 1968.

2006—Ohio State beats Michigan 42–39 in Ohio Stadium in a No. 1–versus–No. 2 showdown to finish the regular season 12–0.

2007—The favored Buckeyes are blown out by No. 2 Florida 41–14 in the national championship game in the Fiesta Bowl.

2008—Tressel leads OSU to their second straight national championship game, where they lose to No. 2 LSU 38–24 in New Orleans.

2010—In his first Rose Bowl as a head coach, the Buckeyes defeat Oregon 26–17 to finish the season at 11–2 and ranked No. 5 in the country.

MARCH 7, 2011—Yahoo Sports reports Tressel knew of potential violations involving his players in April 2010,

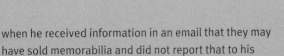

when he received information in an email that they may
have sold memorabilia and did not report that to his
bosses or Ohio State's compliance office.

MARCH 8, 2011—Ohio State announces at a news conference
that it discovered Tressel's major NCAA violations while
checking his emails in January on another matter and is
self-reporting them to the NCAA. The news conference
with Tressel, Smith, and OSU President Gordon Gee is
generally viewed as poorly handled, with Gee's joke
about Tressel's job status—"I'm just hoping the coach
doesn't dismiss me"—serving to hover over the rest of
this situation. Tressel is fined $250,000 and suspended
for two games by Ohio State.

MARCH 11, 2011—Columbus attorney Chris Cicero,
who informed Tressel in emails about his players'
memorabilia sales and association with a suspected
drug trafficker, tells ESPN the first players he told
Tressel about were Terrelle Pryor and DeVier Posey.

MARCH 14, 2011—At his first public appearance since the
announcement of sanctions, Tressel, at a banquet in
Canton, says, "I sincerely apologize for what we've
been through." Part of his punishment includes a public
apology, which he was supposed to deliver at the initial
news conference but did not.

MARCH 17, 2011—After the NCAA denies Ohio State's
appeal to reduce the five-game suspensions for five
players, Tressel's suspension is increased from two
games to five at his request, according to Ohio State.

MARCH 25, 2011—Though previously known to Ohio State,
the fact that Tressel emailed Pryor mentor Ted Sarniak
about the potential violations committed by Pryor, while
not informing anyone at Ohio State, is revealed through
a release of emails following a public records request.

MARCH 30, 2011—On the HBO show *Real Sports*, former OSU recruiting target and Auburn player Stanley McClover says he was given money by OSU boosters on a recruiting visit eight years earlier.

MARCH 31, 2011—At a news conference on the day before spring practice, Ohio State announces that assistant Luke Fickell will serve as the interim coach in Tressel's absence. Asked if he considered resigning, Tressel says, "Never had that thought," adding he'd only do it if he thought it best for his players. Meanwhile, at a news conference at the Final Four, new NCAA President Mark Emmert calls a lack of integrity the greatest threat to college athletics, which some view as an ominous sign for Tressel.

APRIL 2, 2011—Oregon State President Ed Ray, a former OSU provost involved with Tressel's hiring, tells the *Plain Dealer*—confirming previous quotes—how serious the Tressel matter is, "Everyone makes mistakes, but if people aren't forthright, then the system isn't going to work." NCAA expert, lawyer, and former Committee on Infractions chairman Gene Marsh says Tressel could survive the situation because of his previously good reputation. Marsh is later hired as Tressel's lawyer.

APRIL 4, 2011—Two pairs of Ohio State gold pants, the trinket awarded for beating Michigan, are sold on the popular History Channel TV series *Pawn Stars*.

APRIL 18, 2011—Golfing legend and former OSU student Jack Nicklaus expresses a belief held by a segment of the Ohio State fan base that Tressel "took the hit" for others with his NCAA violations, though Nicklaus admits that's just his opinion.

APRIL 25, 2011—The NCAA's Notice of Allegations to Ohio State is released, setting July 5 as Ohio State's deadline to respond to the notice and August 12 as the date for Ohio State's hearing in Indianapolis before the NCAA Committee on Infractions.

APRIL 28, 2011—Big Ten Commissioner Jim Delany tells reporters in New Orleans that if it had been known in December that Tressel had previous knowledge of his players' violations, neither Delany nor OSU AD Smith would have asked the NCAA to allow the suspended Buckeyes to play in the Sugar Bowl. Ohio State also releases the original letter it received from the Department of Justice.

MAY 7, 2011—A *Columbus Dispatch* story reveals that players and their families may have received discounted cars from a Columbus dealership, charges which Ohio State says it will investigate.

MAY 13, 2011—Tressel's hiring of Marsh as his lawyer becomes known.

MAY 18, 2011—To illustrate a story on the scandalous year in college sports, *ESPN The Magazine* puts a red sweater vest, Tressel's trademark, on its cover, with the word "Busted" in place of the Ohio State logo.

MAY 26, 2011—Former OSU receiver Ray Small tells *The Lantern*, Ohio State's student newspaper, that he committed NCAA violations by selling Big Ten championship rings while an OSU player, and that when it came to receiving extra benefits such as cash for memorabilia or discounted cars, "Everybody was doing it."

MAY 27, 2011—After strong reaction from current and former OSU players that there was not a culture of violations at Ohio State, Small says his words were mischaracterized and that while he sold rings, he didn't know of other players who did. The *Lantern* stands by its story. Also, Edward Rife, the tattoo parlor owner at the center of the OSU scandal, has his drug and money-laundering charges revealed in U.S. District Court, with a court date set for June 28. He could face five years in prison.

MAY 30, 2011—Jim Tressel resigns as Ohio State's football coach

OHIO STATE

1

GAMES WE HATE

HEADING INTO THE 2011 SEASON, Ohio State is on a seven-game winning streak against Michigan, although, as we all know, these things are cyclical. Each team has had stretches where it has dominated the other, and some of the games stand out more than most. Here are a few that caused heartbreak, sadness, and fits of anger—sometimes all within the same game—among Michigan fans.

1968*

MICHIGAN	7	7	0	0	**14**
OHIO STATE	7	14	6	23	**50**

This is one of a few games that will have an asterisk next to it because, yeah, we hated it, but there was a silver lining.

This was the infamous game in which an Ohio State team en route to the national championship, pulled away from a 21–14 halftime edge by scoring 29 unanswered points in the second half to take a 50–14 victory. There was no doubt OSU was dominant on this day. The Buckeyes outgained the Wolverines in total yardage, 567–311, as fullback Jim Otis led the way with four touchdowns and 143 rushing yards. Quarterback

Rex Kern ran for two TDs, completed five-of-eight passes for 41 yards, and rushed for another 96 yards.

All in all, it appeared it was just your run-of-the-mill shellacking. Happens all the time in sports and it happened on this day. But, late in the game, after Ohio State scored its final touchdown of the day with three minutes remaining, Woody Hayes decided to go for a two-point conversion. The move was shocking, especially for its time. While today it's commonplace for teams to run up 50-, 60-, and 70-point games to get the pretty victory for the BCS standings, in the late 1960s college football—indeed, much of sports—was being played in a gentlemanly fashion.

Running up the score was considered taboo.

Yet, there was Hayes, in all his childish glory, deciding to go for the two-point conversion. Some have speculated that the move was made to try to match OSU's largest margin of victory ever in the series (which was 38 in the 1935 game, thus a two-point conversion would have made the score 52–14 and tied the mark). In reality, though, it was just Woody being his nasty, surly self. Whatever the reason, after the game, Hayes was asked why he went for two in such a situation, and he defiantly responded, "Because I couldn't go for three."

Yup, he truly was a nasty SOB. Ohio State went on to the Rose Bowl and defeated Southern Cal 27–16, claiming the top spot in both major polls and earning the national championship. Ironically, Hayes considered his 1969 team, a year later, to be his greatest team of all-time, and the Buckeyes were looking at back-to-back national titles. But—silver lining alert!—karma is a bitch, and Hayes got his ass bitten. During the off-season between '68 and '69, Michigan hired a former Hayes player and assistant, Glenn E. "Bo" Schembechler, away from Miami of Ohio to become the Wolverines' head coach. Schembechler's team pulled a stunning 24–12 upset of No. 1 Ohio State in the 1969 game, denying the Buckeyes a chance to go to the Rose Bowl and win a second consecutive national championship.

Serves him right.

1973*

OHIO STATE	0	10	0	0	10
MICHIGAN	0	0	3	7	10

This was a classic.

Both teams entered the game unbeaten and, as usual, the game would decide the Big Ten championship, the Rose Bowl participant, and the likely national championship contender.

Ohio State built a 10–0 halftime lead in the game, but in a key sequence in the third quarter, the Buckeyes decided to go for it on fourth-and-2 at the Michigan 34-yard line. Michigan made the big defensive stop and turned it into a field goal to cut the deficit to 10–3.

In the fourth quarter, the Wolverines finally broke through and scored on a fourth-and-1 play from the OSU 10-yard line on a scramble by quarterback Dennis Franklin, tying the game with 9:32 to play. The gut-wrenching part of this is that Michigan had two field-goal attempts in the final 61 seconds—albeit

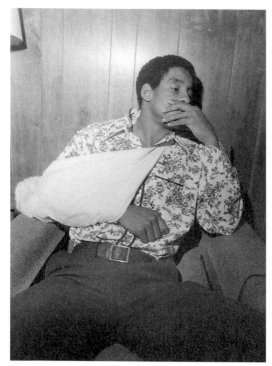

Quarterback Dennis Franklin stares at a television in his Ann Arbor apartment and listens to the report that Ohio State was picked by the Big Ten to appear in the 1973 Rose Bowl. Franklin suffered a broken collarbone during The Game after scoring the tying touchdown. The fact that undefeated Michigan was forced to sit out the postseason changed future Big Ten rules.

long ones—and missed both, or the Wolverines could have won outright. Instead, it ended in a 10–10 tie.

Problem: at the time, only one team from a conference could go to a bowl game. By Big Ten rule, that left it in the hands of the conference's athletics directors, who would vote by secret ballot and select the conference champion and Rose Bowl participant. The prevailing sentiment was that since Michigan had played far better in the second half of the game, and that Ohio State had gone to the Rose Bowl the year before, the ADs would send the Wolverines to Pasadena. But in a 6–4 vote, it was Ohio State going back to Cali.

Afterward, some speculated that when Franklin broke his collarbone on the game-tying touchdown run, the ADs figured he was done and that Ohio State would have the better chance to win the Rose Bowl.

"I was devastated," Franklin told *USA Today* in a 2006 interview. "I remember Bo Schembechler coming into the meeting, trying to explain why we weren't going to the Rose Bowl. But he couldn't explain it."

As for the injury, Franklin said he was more than healthy and ready to go by New Year's Day and, in fact, "The AP sent a reporter to my home in Massillon, Ohio, and took a picture of me throwing a snowball."

But—silver lining alert!—the game did effect some change. To have an unbeaten Michigan team sitting home from the bowl games because of the rules of the day seemed ludicrous, and that quickly changed so that more than one team could participate in postseason play.

2006

MICHIGAN	7	7	10	15	**39**
OHIO STATE	7	21	7	7	**42**

The Game of the Century. Well, one of them, anyway.

It was a game that matched unbeaten and No. 1–ranked Ohio State against unbeaten and No. 2–ranked Michigan. Hard to believe, but it marked the first time in the history of the grand rivalry that teams came into the game ranked first and second in the country. The stakes were clear—the winner would capture the Big Ten championship and land in the BCS Championship Game.

But before either team took the field, the game was tinged with sadness. Bo Schembechler, Ohio State graduate and Michigan coach, collapsed and died on Friday morning while filming his regular weekly television segment. Before the game the next afternoon, before a then-record crowd of 105,708 at Ohio Stadium, a pregame video tribute to Schembechler was played on the Ohio Stadium scoreboard as the public address announcer read, "Michigan has lost a coach and patriarch. The Big Ten has lost a legend and icon. Ohio State has lost an alumnus and friend."

Michigan took the opening kickoff and drove 80 yards to take a 7–0 lead, which turned out to be their only advantage of the day. Ohio State roared to a 28–14 halftime advantage and led 42–31 late in the game when Chad Henne threw a 16-yard touchdown pass to Tyler Ecker and then a two-point conversion to Steve Breaston to pull the Wolverines within three with 2:16 remaining.

But Michigan could not recover the onside kick, and OSU ran out the clock to secure the victory. Buckeyes quarterback Troy Smith secured the Heisman Trophy by throwing for 316 yards, four touchdowns, and just one interception.

"There were a lot of good playmakers out there today," Ohio State coach Jim Tressel said after the game. "It was a fast-break game the whole way."

A Michigan fan holds up a sign during the 2006 game against No. 1–ranked Ohio State. Alas, the No. 2 Wolverines couldn't overcome their grief and squeeze out a win for Bo Schembechler, who had died the day before.

Too much of a fast-break game for Michigan coach Lloyd Carr, who said, "We gave up too many big plays. Those are mistakes in a game like this, in any game, that will get you beat."

After the game, there were a couple of weeks of specula-tion that the two teams would—should?—meet again in the national championship game. After all, there was no other team who had dominated the regular season like the Buckeyes and Wolverines did. But after a once-beaten Florida team won the SEC crown, it was the Gators, not U-M, that was invited to play unbeaten Ohio State for the national title.

Florida won easily, 41–14; Michigan settled for the Rose Bowl but lost to USC 32–18.

2002

MICHIGAN	3	6	0	0	9
OHIO STATE	7	0	0	7	14

Another in a long line of games in which the outcome not only would decide the conference championship, but also Ohio State's appearance in the national title game.

Michigan was 9–2 coming into Ohio Stadium, and the Buckeyes were undefeated. Michigan went ahead 3–0 midway through the opening period, but Ohio State took the lead on a two-yard TD run by Maurice Clarett, its questionable and shifty—and not in a good way—freshman sensation.

Michigan added two second-quarter field goals to make it 9–7 Wolverines at halftime, and the crowd was getting the sense that this was going to be yet another "same old, same old," with Michigan ruining yet another OSU chance at a national championship. But with the score still the same, the Buckeyes took over at their own 37 with 8:40 remaining and drove 63 yards for the score, with Maurice Hall taking a pitch and doing the honors from three yards out to go up 14–9.

The Wolverines eventually got the ball back at their own 20-yard line with 56 seconds left and drove to the OSU 24 with just one second on the clock. But John Navarre's pass to Braylon Edwards was intercepted by Will Allen to end the game.

"We knew it was going to be a slugfest. Anyone who thought it was going to be anything other than a game decided at the end hasn't been around the Ohio State–Michigan game," said Tressel.

The victory, of course, put the Buckeyes into the national championship game against No. 1 Miami, where...

2003: Fiesta Bowl, National Championship (2OT)

OHIO STATE	0	14	3	0	7	7	31
MIAMI	7	0	7	3	7	0	24

No, this wasn't a Michigan–Ohio State game, but it's a game we hate because the Buckeyes won a flawed national championship that they had no business winning.

That was *not* pass interference. Bottom line.

Let's cut right to the chase. Miami up 24–17 in OT, OSU facing a fourth-and-3 at the Miami 5-yard line to stay alive. Buckeyes quarterback Craig Krenzel dropped back, looked to his right, and sent a pass toward Chris Gamble. Gamble couldn't come up with it, and the ball fell to the ground. Hurricanes players streamed onto the field. Fireworks went off in the stadium. Krenzel had taken his helmet off and slumped to the ground. All this happened *before* the official decided to throw a flag.

More than three seconds elapsed after the sideline official, who was in perfect position and was looking at the play, waved it

OSU's Chris Gamble (7) can't make a touchdown reception at the back of the end zone as Miami's Glen Sharpe tackles him. That's okay, though, since Sharpe got called for pass interference. Even the ABC announcers thought this was a bad call.

incomplete. Then Terry Porter's flag came flying in from the back of the end zone. Pass interference on Glenn Sharpe. Um, why? No. 1, the sideline official had the best look at it (check the replays) and ruled it incomplete. The ABC announcers on replay were screaming, "Bad call! Bad call!" No. 2, why did it take so long for Porter to throw the flag? He said it was because he wanted to make sure he had it right in his mind. Uh, if there was indecision, why even throw the flag on fourth down in overtime of the national championship game?

Some Buckeyes have said the penalty actually happened before the two players reached the end zone, when Sharpe jammed Gamble at the line of scrimmage. Fair enough. There was contact. But, again, the sideline official, who had the best view, didn't call a penalty. The flag came flying from Porter in the back of the end zone. So if the penalty was at the line of scrimmage, why didn't the flag come immediately at that moment?

Frankly, if you watch the replays, Gamble blew it. He should have caught the football. Krenzel made a nice pass, and Gamble just muffed it.

The 2002 national championship was a tainted title for Ohio State. It's okay, Buckeyes fans. You can admit it. And if it wasn't tainted because of the "pass interference" call, then it was tainted simply by having used Maurice Clarett all season.

1970

MICHIGAN	0	3	6	0	**9**
OHIO STATE	3	7	0	10	**20**

In yet another battle of two undefeated teams—see the pattern here and why the rivalry is so great?—Ohio State came into the game 8–0 and ranked fifth in the nation while Michigan was 9–0 and ranked fourth.

The game began with Michigan fumbling the opening kickoff. Ohio State recovered and quickly went ahead 3–0, but U-M tied the game on the first play of the second quarter. Rex Kern hit Bruce Jankowski for a 26-yard TD to put OSU ahead at halftime 10–3. Michigan scored a touchdown in the third quarter and appeared ready to tie the game, but the Buckeyes' Tim Anderson blocked the extra point. The momentum boost carried through the rest of the game as OSU added a field goal and four-yard TD run by Leo Hayden to win 20–9.

Interesting note: Hayden was one of four Ohio State players chosen in the first round of the NFL Draft in 1971, along with John Brockington, Jack Tatum, and William Anderson.

1992

MICHIGAN	0	6	7	0	13
OHIO STATE	3	0	0	10	13

Ohio State president E. Gordon Gee made himself look like a fool in early 2011 when, during a press conference in which Tressel admitted he covered up Tattoo Gate and never told his superiors when he first learned of the incidents, Gee was asked if he considered firing the coach. He responded by saying, "I'm just hopeful the coach doesn't dismiss me."

Riiiiiight.

Well, it wasn't the first time Gee said something ridiculously stupid. In the 1992 game Ohio State coach John Cooper entered the Michigan contest having not beaten the Wolverines in four previous tries. When the Buckeyes, playing

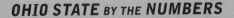

OHIO STATE *by the* NUMBERS

ALL-TIME RECORD VS. MICHIGAN: 44–57–6

BIGGEST MARGIN OF VICTORY VS. MICHIGAN:
38 points (38–0), 1935

WORST DEFEAT VS. MICHIGAN: 86 points (86–0), 1902

LONGEST CONSECUTIVE WIN STREAK VS. MICHIGAN:
Seven (2004–2010)

LONGEST CONSECUTIVE LOSING STREAK VS. MICHIGAN:
Nine (1901–1909)

CONFERENCE TITLES: 35

HOME RECORD VS. MICHIGAN: 24–27–2

AWAY RECORD VS. MICHIGAN: 20–30–4

PF: 1,475

PA: 1,753

OHIO STATE

at home, scored a touchdown with less than five minutes remaining in the game, OSU was within 13–12 and facing a critical decision—go for the two-point conversion and the likely win or kick the extra point to tie the game and hope you get the ball back.

Cooper opted for the latter, later saying, "With over four minutes to play, it [a two-point conversion] never crossed my mind. The idea was to hold them, get the ball back, and kick a winning field goal."

Well, OSU got the ball back all right and got to Michigan's 49-yard line with 88 seconds remaining and faced a fourth-and-4. But instead of pressing on with the drive and moving into field-goal position, Cooper elected to punt the ball, and the game ended in a tie. Cooper caught a lot of heat for playing for the tie, but not from his president. After the game, Gee said, "It was one of our greatest wins."

Pardon? Yes, the Wolverines came into the game unbeaten at 8–0–2, so it was probably satisfying to slap yet another tie on them. But "one of our greatest wins?" Are ya kiddin'?

So why do we hate this game? Well, we're not quite sure if it's because Gee's comments give us pause to wonder how he's in charge of a major university or if it's because it's simply emblematic of the overall idiocy that permeates the Ohio State campus and the greater Columbus metropolis.

1979

OHIO STATE	0	6	6	6	**18**
MICHIGAN	0	7	8	0	**15**

This was Earle Bruce's first year as the Ohio State coach, and the victory at Michigan Stadium wrapped up an undefeated regular season for the Buckeyes. The game itself wasn't terribly exciting on either side. Michigan (8–2 entering the game) started a freshman quarterback in Rich Hewlett who had taken just four snaps all year, and he went out with an injury during the game. Ohio Stated started Art Schlichter—insert your own gambling joke here—and he threw for 196 yards in the victory.

What was notable, however, was what happened after the game—OSU fans rioted. Now that, in and of itself, isn't exactly newsworthy. Buckeyes fans are genetically predisposed to the effects of alcohol. That is, they can't handle it. They can't hold their liquor. A couple of bottles of beer, and they're done for the night. OSU frat boys have been drunk under the table by girls from Ursuline College. When an OSU student goes into his future place of employment at 7-Eleven to buy a 24-pack, the guy at the counter automatically thinks, *What, you and your 11 friends gonna get drunk tonight?*

So, fueled by the two Coors Lights they each snuck in the parking lot prior to the game and the OSU victory, Buckeyes fans rioted after the game. What was noteworthy was that the game was at Michigan Stadium! Yeah, the idiots decided they would overturn some cars, set one on fire, throw some firecrackers and cherry bombs, and break some glass...in Ann Arbor. According to the fine folks who wrote that other book about their love for that school down south, police arrested more than 300 students.

1934

MICHIGAN	0	0	0	0	**0**
OHIO STATE	6	6	0	22	**34**

Interestingly enough, this is where one of the most infamous clichés in sports—and elsewhere, for that matter—may have been first uttered, and this is the game where one of the dumbest traditions in college football started.

By 1934, U-M had already asserted its dominance in The Game, winning 22 and tying two of the first 30 games. So, in a move that would become commonplace for Ohio State,

OHIO STATE

MICHIGAN'S FIRST LOSS TO OSU

Michigan began its rivalry against the Buckeyes by going 15 consecutive games without a loss—a streak of 13 victories and two ties between 1897 and 1918 (after the series began in 1897, there were no Michigan-OSU games played in 1898–1899, and from 1913 through 1917).

Alas, all good things must come to an end, and on October 25, 1919, it did for the Wolverines.

As described in the November 1919 edition of the *Ohio State Monthly*, "On October 25 was accomplished that which made the heart of every alumnus joyous—the defeat of Michigan at football. Accompanied by 3,500 rooters, about half of whom were alumni, the Buckeyes invaded Ann Arbor and returned a 13–3 count against the clan of Yost. The Maize and Blue had no excuse to offer, as the Michigan team was one of the strongest ever put out at Ann Arbor and was in good trim at the start. The Wolverines were fortunate to escape with the score as low as it was, for they were completely outclassed after the first period, failing to make a first down in the last three quarters and making but one in the entire game."

the school hired a coach they thought could beat Michigan. Francis A. Schmidt took over in '34 as the Buckeyes' new coach, and according to legend his first speech to the team went something like this:

My name's Schmidt. I'm the new football coach here. This thing is a football. At one time, it was used here at Ohio State to place behind opponents' goal lines, for which Ohio State was credited with six points. I understand that usage has been sort of overlooked here in recent years. That's not funny. That's tragic. For your information, I'm figuring on reviving the old custom. And one more thing. I want you to remember it from now on: we're going to beat Michigan this year. Yes, beat Michigan. Why not? Those guys put their pants on one leg at a time, the same as you do.

Now, frankly, we know lots of people who like to sit on the edge of the bed or a chair or whatever and slide their pants on both legs at the same time. Just sayin'.

What happened next, though, was a little weird. Apparently riffing off of Schmidt's "one leg at a time" comment, the tradition of awarding Golden Pants medallions to OSU players who beat Michigan began. Officially, the Ohio Pants Club— no, we're not making this up—was formed in April 1935 by a bunch of Columbus businessmen. Of course, it can't be that big of a deal since the golden pants were among the items Terrelle Pryor and his buddies hawked in 2010.

As for Schmidt's cliché…okay, we'll give him that. Then again, here's some clichés we'd use *way* before ever uttering, "Those guys put their pants on one leg at a time, the same as you do":

> We're taking it one game at a time.
> He has to step up here.
> He's playing like a senior.

He gives 110 percent.

We gotta make plays.

No use crying over spilled milk.

If you can't stand the heat, get out of the kitchen.

A rolling stone gathers no moss.

We have to take it to the next level.

They just wanted it more.

Our backs were against the wall.

We needed to make a statement today.

We overcame a tremendous amount of adversity.

You don't throw the baby out with the bathwater.

It's a game of inches.

He has a cannon for an arm.

He zigged when he should have zagged.

He hit him right between the numbers.

There's no "I" in team. (But there is "me.")

All's well that ends well.

It's not over 'til the fat lady sings.

What goes around comes around.

He got his just desserts (like Woody Hayes in the '69 game.)

2004

MICHIGAN	14	0	0	7	**21**
OHIO STATE	7	13	14	3	**37**

2005

OHIO STATE	6	6	0	13	**25**
MICHIGAN	0	7	11	3	**21**

2006

MICHIGAN	7	7	10	15	**39**
OHIO STATE	7	21	7	7	**42**

2007

OHIO STATE	0	7	7	0	**14**
MICHIGAN	3	0	0	0	**3**

2008

MICHIGAN	0	7	0	0	**7**
OHIO STATE	7	7	14	14	**42**

2009

OHIO STATE	7	7	7	0	**21**
MICHIGAN	0	3	7	0	**10**

2010

MICHIGAN	0	7	0	0	**7**
OHIO STATE	0	24	13	0	**37**

We lump these seven games together for obvious reasons.

When Michigan won the 100th game of this great rivalry in 2003, it marked the last time the Wolverines have beaten Ohio State. It's been seven years and seven games of futility since that time, including, surprisingly, four straight losses by coach Lloyd Carr, who had a winning record against the Buckeyes until the 2004 game seemed to turn the tide.

What makes the losses part of the hate brigade is just knowing what kind of program OSU is running down there.

But, as we said, these things are cyclical. It will turn around. For a reminder of that, and of Michigan's dominance in the rivalry, just check out the all-time scores.

Michigan vs. Ohio State All-Time Series Scores

(italics denotes Michigan victory)

1897	*Michigan 34, Ohio State 0 (at Ann Arbor)*
1900	Michigan 0, Ohio State 0 (at Ann Arbor)
1901	*Michigan 21, Ohio State 0 (at Columbus)*
1902	*Michigan 86, Ohio State 0 (at Ann Arbor)*
1903	*Michigan 36, Ohio State 0 (at Ann Arbor)*
1904	*Michigan 31, Ohio State 6 (at Columbus)*
1905	*Michigan 40, Ohio State 0 (at Ann Arbor)*
1906	*Michigan 6, Ohio State 0 (at Columbus)*
1907	*Michigan 22, Ohio State 0 (at Ann Arbor)*
1908	*Michigan 10, Ohio State 6 (at Columbus)*
1909	*Michigan 33, Ohio State 6 (at Ann Arbor)*
1910	Michigan 3, Ohio State 3 (at Columbus)
1911	*Michigan 19, Ohio State 0 (at Ann Arbor)*
1912	*Michigan 14, Ohio State 0 (at Columbus)*
1918	*Michigan 14, Ohio State 0 (at Columbus)*
1919	Michigan 3, Ohio State 13 (at Ann Arbor)
1920	Michigan 7, Ohio State 14 (at Columbus)
1921	Michigan 0, Ohio State 14 (at Ann Arbor)
1922	*Michigan 19, Ohio State 0 (at Columbus)*
1923	*Michigan 23, Ohio State 0 (at Ann Arbor)*
1924	*Michigan 16, Ohio State 6 (at Columbus)*
1925	*Michigan 10, Ohio State 0 (at Ann Arbor)*

1926	Michigan 17, Ohio State 16 (at Columbus)
1927	Michigan 21, Ohio State 0 (at Ann Arbor)
1928	Michigan 7, Ohio State 19 (at Columbus)
1929	Michigan 0, Ohio State 7 (at Ann Arbor)
1930	Michigan 13, Ohio State 0 (at Columbus)
1931	Michigan 0, Ohio State 7 (at Ann Arbor)
1932	Michigan 14, Ohio State 10 (at Columbus)
1933	Michigan 13, Ohio State 0 (at Ann Arbor)
1934	Michigan 0, Ohio State 34 (at Columbus)
1935	Michigan 0, Ohio State 38 (at Ann Arbor)
1936	Michigan 0, Ohio State 21 (at Columbus)
1937	Michigan 0, Ohio State 21 (at Ann Arbor)
1938	Michigan 18, Ohio State 0 (at Columbus)
1939	Michigan 21, Ohio State 0 (at Ann Arbor)
1940	Michigan 40, Ohio State 0 (at Columbus)
1941	Michigan 20, Ohio State 20 (at Ann Arbor)
1942	Michigan 7, Ohio State 21 (at Columbus)
1943	Michigan 45, Ohio State 7 (at Ann Arbor)
1944	Michigan 14, Ohio State 18 (at Columbus)
1945	Michigan 7, Ohio State 3 (at Ann Arbor)
1946	Michigan 58, Ohio State 6 (at Columbus)
1947	Michigan 21, Ohio State 0 (at Ann Arbor)
1948	Michigan 13, Ohio State 3 (at Columbus)
1949	Michigan 7, Ohio State 7 (at Ann Arbor)
1950	Michigan 9, Ohio State 3 (at Columbus)
1951	Michigan 7, Ohio State 0 (at Ann Arbor)
1952	Michigan 7, Ohio State 27 (at Columbus)
1953	Michigan 20, Ohio State 0 (at Ann Arbor)
1954	Michigan 7, Ohio State 21 (at Columbus)
1955	Michigan 0, Ohio State 17 (at Ann Arbor)
1956	Michigan 19, Ohio State 0 (at Columbus)
1957	Michigan 14, Ohio State 31 (at Ann Arbor)

1958	Michigan 14, Ohio State 20 (at Columbus)
1959	*Michigan 23, Ohio State 14 (at Ann Arbor)*
1960	Michigan 0, Ohio State 7 (at Columbus)
1961	Michigan 20, Ohio State 50 (at Ann Arbor)
1962	Michigan 0, Ohio State 28 (at Columbus)
1963	Michigan 10, Ohio State 14 (at Ann Arbor)
1964	*Michigan 10, Ohio State 0 (at Columbus)*
1965	Michigan 7, Ohio State 9 (at Ann Arbor)
1966	*Michigan 17, Ohio State 3 (at Columbus)*
1967	Michigan 14, Ohio State 24 (at Ann Arbor)
1968	Michigan 14, Ohio State 50 (at Columbus)
1969	*Michigan 24, Ohio State 12 (at Ann Arbor)*
1970	Michigan 9, Ohio State 20 (at Columbus)
1971	*Michigan 10, Ohio State 7 (at Ann Arbor)*
1972	Michigan 11, Ohio State 14 (at Columbus)
1973	Michigan 10, Ohio State 10 (at Ann Arbor)
1974	Michigan 10, Ohio State 12 (at Columbus)
1975	Michigan 14, Ohio State 21 (at Ann Arbor)
1976	*Michigan 22, Ohio State 0 (at Columbus)*
1977	*Michigan 14, Ohio State 6 (at Ann Arbor)*
1978	*Michigan 14, Ohio State 3 (at Columbus)*
1979	Michigan 15, Ohio State 18 (at Ann Arbor)
1980	*Michigan 9, Ohio State 3 (at Columbus)*
1981	Michigan 9, Ohio State 14 (at Ann Arbor)
1982	Michigan 14, Ohio State 24 (at Columbus)
1983	*Michigan 24, Ohio State 21 (at Ann Arbor)*
1984	Michigan 6, Ohio State 21 (at Columbus)
1985	*Michigan 27, Ohio State 17 (at Ann Arbor)*
1986	*Michigan 26, Ohio State 24 (at Columbus)*
1987	Michigan 20, Ohio State 23 (at Ann Arbor)
1988	*Michigan 34, Ohio State 31 (at Columbus)*
1989	*Michigan 28, Ohio State 18 (at Ann Arbor)*

1990	*Michigan 16, Ohio State 13 (at Columbus)*
1991	*Michigan 31, Ohio State 3 (at Ann Arbor)*
1992	Michigan 13, Ohio State 13 (at Columbus)
1993	*Michigan 28, Ohio State 0 (at Ann Arbor)*
1994	Michigan 6, Ohio State 22 (at Columbus)
1995	*Michigan 31, Ohio State 23 (at Ann Arbor)*
1996	*Michigan 13, Ohio State 9 (at Columbus)*
1997	*Michigan 20, Ohio State 14 (at Ann Arbor)*
1998	Michigan 16, Ohio State 31 (at Columbus)
1999	*Michigan 24, Ohio State 17 (at Ann Arbor)*
2000	*Michigan 38, Ohio State 26 (at Columbus)*
2001	Michigan 20, Ohio State 26 (at Ann Arbor)
2002	Michigan 9, Ohio State 14 (at Columbus)
2003	*Michigan 35, Ohio State 21 (at Ann Arbor)*
2004	Michigan 21, Ohio State 37 (at Columbus)
2005	Michigan 21, Ohio State 25 (at Ann Arbor)
2006	Michigan 39, Ohio State 42 (at Columbus)
2007	Michigan 3, Ohio State 14 (at Ann Arbor)
2008	Michigan 7, Ohio State 42 (at Columbus)
2009	Michigan 10, Ohio State 21 (at Ann Arbor)
2010	Michigan 7, Ohio State 37 (at Columbus)

2

PLAYERS WE HATE

THIS IS, OF COURSE, in no particular order. We hate all OSU players equally.

GREG HARE AND RICK MIDDLETON

In the great lore of Ohio State football, Greg Hare and Rick Middleton aren't exactly Archie Griffin and Eddie George. And, to be frank and to be honest, the grainy footage from the 1973 game between Michigan and Ohio State doesn't necessarily show the duo to be the ringleaders for what I'm about to tell you.

It was the radio call by Michigan announcer Bob Ufer, though, that singled out the two.

As any Michigan fan knows, the M Club boosters hold up their famous "Go Blue" banner prior to every game, and the Wolverines come racing out of the tunnel of Michigan Stadium to head to their sideline, running under the banner and leaping to tap it for luck.

On this day, as Ohio State was introduced first, the Buckeyes came out of the tunnel and headed toward the banner. And, well, let Ufer take it from there.

> Here they come: Hare, Middleton, and the Buckeyes… and…and they're tearing down Michigan's coveted M Club banner! They will meet a dastardly fate here for that! There isn't a Michigan Man who wouldn't like to go out and scalp those Buckeyes right now. They had the *audacity*, the *unmitigated gall*, to tear down the coveted "M" that Michigan's going to run out from under!…But the M-men will prevail because they're getting the banner back up again. And here they [the Michigan team] come! The maize and blue! Take it away, 105,000 fans!"

Yup, the cads from Columbus tried to tear down and stomp the banner. You stay classy, OSU.

ARCHIE GRIFFIN

In 1974 Ohio State tailback Archie Griffin became just the fifth junior ever to win the Heisman Trophy.

And then a year later he made history.

In 1975 Griffin became the first player ever to win a second Heisman, and to this day remains the only two-time winner of college football's most coveted individual award. Griffin, now the president and CEO of the Ohio State Alumni Association, was the Buckeyes' starting tailback for four years, leading Ohio State to a 40–5–1 record and four Big Ten titles between 1972 and 1975. He started in four consecutive Rose Bowls—one of the only two players ever to do so—and was a three-time, first-team All-American.

What's to hate about that?

Well, how about this—Griffin went 3–0–1 against Michigan during his career. Asked by the *Michigan Daily* in 2009 what his favorite Michigan–Ohio State game was, Griffin said:

> Probably the last one we played at Michigan, 1975, because we were tied for the Big Ten, and Michigan had to beat us in order to go to the Rose Bowl.... And they were beating us—they were beating us pretty good. I think they were ahead 14–7 with four minutes to go. And I'll never forget at that time…when the offense went out on the field, we thought this might be our last shot. [Ohio State quarterback Cornelius Greene] called the players together, and we held hands in the huddle and said a little prayer, and just asked the Lord to give us strength to play the type of football we're capable of playing. We went out there and started moving the football. Scored a touchdown, tied it up 14–14. Michigan probably got a little desperate because a tie would have kept us in the Rose Bowl, and they started passing the football and threw an interception to my younger brother, [Ohio State cornerback] Ray [Griffin]. And Ray took it down to about the 4- or 5-yard line, and we took it over again for another touchdown, and we ended up winning the game 21–14. And that really stands out in my mind, and it shouldn't stand out in my mind, because I had a streak of 31 straight 100-yard games going on, and Michigan stopped me from getting 100 yards that day. But the fact we won that game trumped the fact that I didn't get the 100 yards.

Archie Griffin dashes toward the end zone during a game against Illinois on November 2, 1974, in Columbus. The 22-yard run put Griffin over the 100-yards rushing mark for the 18th straight game, setting one of the two-time Heisman Trophy winner's many college records.

One thing we do like about Griffin is his appreciation of The Game.

"When people ask you about the games you played in and what-not, they don't usually ask about many of the other schools in the Big Ten," he said. "But the one you can be sure that they're going to ask about is Michigan. How did you do against Michigan? I'm proud to say that I never lost to Michigan. And that's something that I say, and I'm very, very proud of that."

Griffin, of course, played for Woody Hayes, and we all know how Hayes felt about the Michigan game. As Griffin recalled:

> During the course of the whole week before the Michigan game, he'd certainly have former players come in and talk with us about their experience with the Michigan game. And the players that he would bring in were pretty emotional about that experience, and it came through when they would talk to the team. And one particular instance on my first Michigan week that we had happened with a guy by the name of Dave Whitfield [Ohio State defensive end, 1967–1969].... He got to talk to the team, and tears were coming out of his eyes. And I looked around the room and I saw the look on other players' faces, and I just said, "Wow, I mean, this thing is even bigger than I thought. What have I gotten myself into?" Because it was really an emotional situation, and it was like people were ready to run out that room and play the Michigan game right there on that Monday. And I know that that's not what Coach Hayes wanted at that time, because he likes to get you up gradually for a game—he don't want you to be ready to play that game on Monday, he wants you to be ready to play it on Saturday. But it was very emotional, and it gave me a real feel for what the game was all about. Dave Whitfield did that.

VIC JANOWICZ

Janowicz, a halfback, is one of OSU's six Heisman Trophy winners, taking the award in 1950.

That was a season in which he scored 16 touchdowns and had 875 yards in total offense, a great deal of it coming in one game against Iowa, when he ran for two touchdowns and threw for four more in an 83–21 Ohio State victory, a game in which he also set a Big Ten record with 10 extra points.

Ironically, many pundits believe he wrapped up the Heisman Trophy by converting a 27-yard field goal in blizzard conditions in the famous Snow Bowl game against Michigan in 1950, as well as booting a whopping 21 punts for 685 yards.

Janowicz has been portrayed as one of the greatest all-around players to ever lace 'em up.

But he's no Tom Harmon, so let's not get crazy.

HOWARD "HOPALONG" CASSADY

Okay, he has a pretty cool nickname, we'll give him that.

Cassady was yet another Heisman Trophy winner for the Buckeyes. In four years, Cassady helped the Buckeyes to a 29–8 record and their first of five national championships under Woody Hayes. Cassady also earned many individual honors, including twice being named All-America, winning the 1955 Heisman Trophy, and being named 1955 Associated Press Athlete of the Year. In 2000 he became the third OSU

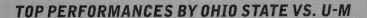

TOP PERFORMANCES BY OHIO STATE VS. U-M

RUSHING YARDS: Chris "Beanie" Wells, 222, 2007

PASSING YARDS: Joe Germaine, 330, 1998

RECEIVING YARDS: David Boston, 217, 1998

RECEPTIONS: Brian Staeblein, 12, 1992

POINTS: Bob Ferguson, 1961; Jim Otis, 1968, both with 24

FIELD GOALS: Tom Klaban, 4, 1974

LONGEST PUNT RETURN: Tom Campana, 85 yards (TD), 1971

INTERCEPTIONS: Fred Bruney, 3, 1952

TOTAL TACKLES: Chris Spielman, 29, 1986

OHIO STATE

player to have his jersey retired, his No. 40 joining Archie Griffin's No. 45 and Vic Janowicz's No. 31 in Ohio Stadium.

From the beginning, Cassady proved despite his small 5'10", 150-pound frame, that he belonged at Ohio State. Coming off the bench as a freshman in the fall of 1952, he scored three touchdowns in the season opener against Indiana.

"I still didn't have a uniform the Thursday before the game," Cassady recalled in 2000. "But, eventually I ended up with No. 40 and was on the bench for the first game. We got down 14–0 at the half. The coaching staff sent me in to play in the third quarter. I scored three touchdowns, and Ohio State went on to win [33–14]."

Cassady was a regular in the lineup from then on. He eventually played in 36 of 37 possible games. In 1955 he was named an All-American after rushing for 958 yards and 15 touchdowns. At the end of the season, he was recognized as the Heisman Trophy winner and the AP Athlete of the Year, just five years after Janowicz won his Heisman.

EDDIE GEORGE

Hate him. Not because of anything he did or said. George was actually one of the few respectful OSU players and a genuinely nice guy even though he wore the scarlet and gray and made the piss-poor choice to play for the Buckeyes.

Hate him because he was so freakin' good.

The 1995 Heisman Trophy winner had his No. 27 retired by OSU, and how many schools saw that coming when they recruited George with the intention of turning him into a linebacker?

"Growing up, I knew I wanted the ball in my hands and to be in a position to carry the ball as much as possible," George told the school's website. "I wanted to be in control. I didn't want to change, and that is why I chose Ohio State. They gave me a chance to run the ball."

John Cooper, former Buckeyes head coach, was the man who made that happen.

"Not many colleges recruited him as a running back," Cooper said. "They all figured he would make a great linebacker. He came here focused and with the goal of becoming a Heisman winner, and he did just that."

George's senior season was phenomenal. He rushed for 1,927 yards in 1995, a school record for a single season, and scored 24 times, the second most for a single season in school history. He also recorded three of the top 15 rushing performances in Ohio State history that year. In the early part of the season George totaled 212 yards against Washington (September 16) before rushing for 207 yards against Notre Dame (September 30). But the game that really got the attention of the rest of the nation was his performance against Illinois on November 11, when he rushed for 314 yards a week before the Michigan game.

"He had an awesome performance against Illinois as a senior," Cooper said. "He ran for 314 yards, and that was not a weak defense. They had a solid defense, and two of their linebackers, Kevin Hardy and Simeon Rice, were drafted in the first round. He proved his dedication to his goals, and the Heisman is proof of that."

"The game in which I ran for 314 yards against Illinois to close my career was ironic because of the trouble I had [against them] as a freshman," George said. "I wasn't concerned with breaking any records. I was trying to help my team win. It was all because I stuck with it and knew I could improve. I made many believers in my ability that year, and they rewarded me with the Heisman."

George was also keenly aware of The Game. "If you walk around this facility, you see signs, 'The countdown to Michigan,' 'What have you done to beat Michigan?'" he told the *Dayton Daily*

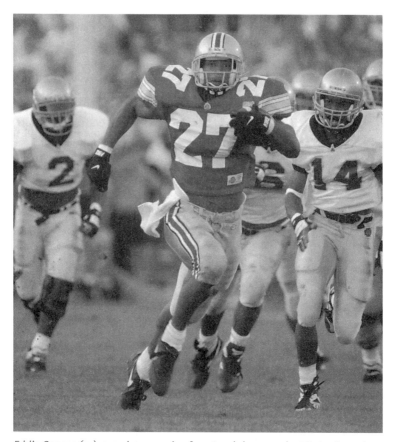

Eddie George (27), seen here running for a touchdown against Notre Dame in 1995, had exceptional talent that he used effectively for Ohio State. That's why we both hate and respect him.

News in 2009. "Everything is directed to that game. It's the Big Ten, then it's Ohio State and the rivalry. That's something kids understand when they come here from Day One."

Alas, while George might have had respect for the rivalry, he nonetheless couldn't beat Michigan, getting just one win against the Wolverines and suffering a pair of losses, including the shocking 31–23 game in 1995 in which he was outshined by U-M's Tim Biakabutuka's 313 yards.

George has done well for himself since his retirement from the NFL. He married Tamara "Taj" Johnson, an R&B singer and contestant on the reality TV show *Survivor*. George made an appearance on *Survivor* with his wife, then the two of them teamed up on the reality show *I Married a Baller*. George has also appeared on *Nash Bridges*, the MTV show *Made*, in the Steven Seagal movie *Into the Sun*, and the Dwayne Johnson movie *The Game Plan*. He hosted a video-game show and has worked with FOX Sports on various pregame shows and as a game analyst. He opened restaurants in Nashville and Columbus (Eddie George's Grille 27). He is also a licensed landscape architect and recently graduated from Northwestern's highly regarded MBA program.

DAVID BOSTON

Ah, David, David, David. What a bust you turned out to be in the NFL. So much talent, so little smarts.

The problem with Boston is, he couldn't keep his mouth shut. And when push came to shove, he couldn't back it up. Prior to the 1997 Michigan–Ohio State game, Boston told reporters, "I play against better defensive backs than [Charles Woodson] in practice every day."

Hmmm. Pretty heady statement, considering that Woodson, to that point, had led Michigan to a 10–0 mark and the No. 1 ranking in the country and was being talked about as a Heisman Trophy candidate even though he was primarily a defensive player.

Of course, we all know the upshot. Woodson owned Boston that day, even though the junior caught a fluke touchdown pass. Michigan won the game 20–14, went on to the Rose Bowl, and completed an undefeated national championship season with a victory over Washington State. Woodson, of course, won the Heisman.

After the game, Woodson said of Boston, "I was like a father out there, chastising his son for talking to the wrong people."

The most iconic image from that 1997 game was the cover of *Sports Illustrated* the following week, with Michigan defensive back Marcus Ray putting Boston on his keister during the game. Ironically, Boston came back with a big game in The Game the following year, with 10 catches for 217 yards and two touchdowns in an Ohio State victory that he mistakenly thought was some sort of measure of revenge for him.

After the game, Boston said, "There were some things said last year after the game, that one of their players was chastising me or something. I didn't really understand the message there. But today, I just went out and proved that I'm human."

Uh, David? The player in question was the Heisman Trophy winner, who was *not* on the field covering you like a blanket in the '98 game like he did in '97 because he left for the National Football League.

Boston was drafted eighth overall by the Arizona Cardinals in the 1999 NFL Draft and spent eight underwhelming seasons in the NFL. Charles Woodson was a NFL Defensive MVP and won a Super Bowl in 2011 with the Green Bay Packers.

TROY SMITH

Smith turned in a big senior season in 2006, good enough to end up as the lesser of four evils. His Heisman Trophy—OSU's sixth and most recent—came against lackluster competition in Arkansas running back Darren McFadden, who finished second, Notre Dame quarterback Brady Quinn, who was third, and fourth-place finisher Steve Slaton of West Virginia.

He led the Buckeyes to a 12–0 regular season mark before the team again was thumped by an SEC team in the national championship game. He threw for a school single-season record 30 touchdowns and became just the second quarterback in Ohio State history to post a 3–0 record against Michigan as a starter. In the No. 1–versus–No. 2 battle, a 42–39 win over the Wolverines, Smith threw four touchdown passes and topped the 300-yard mark in total offense for the third consecutive year against the Wolverines.

JUSTIN BOREN

Listen, we'll be the first to tell you that Rich Rodriguez just didn't get it. Didn't get Michigan, didn't get The Game, didn't get the history, the tradition...he thought he was coaching at just another school like—gasp!—his situation at West Virginia, when, in fact, he never came to grips with or appreciated the fact that he was now coaching at the greatest college football program in the history of the game when he took over for Lloyd Carr in 2008.

So, yeah, RichRod had to go and, mercifully, he was cut loose after Michigan's 52–14 debacle against Mississippi State in the January 1, 2011, Gator Bowl.

All that said, the Justin Boren situation was a classic case of a player not being able to handle transition, change, and some saltier language. Boren was a highly recruited offensive lineman whose father played at U-M under Bo Schembechler. He signed with the Wolverines when Lloyd Carr was the coach, started one game as a freshman, and moved into the starting lineup as a sophomore. When RichRod took over, two things happened. One, he brought his no-huddle spread option offense with him, and that turned out to be a huge problem for Boren. He lasted less than two weeks in spring ball.

But it wasn't just that he left the team. He announced he was transferring to Ohio State—becoming just the third player to ever don both uniforms—and made a statement to the media in which he said, "Michigan football was a family, built on mutual respect and support for each other from Coach Carr on down. We knew it took the entire family, a team effort, and we all worked together…. I have great trouble accepting that those family values have eroded in just a few months…. That I am unable to perform under these circumstances at the level I expect of myself, and my teammates and Michigan fans deserve, is why I have made the decision to leave."

To his credit, Rodriguez let Boren out of his scholarship and allowed him to transfer.

A week after Justin announced his decision, his younger brother, Zach, committed to OSU, saying, "Everyone in the whole family is an Ohio State fan now. No one cares about Michigan at all anymore. That was in the past, and we're all looking forward to being Buckeyes and staying Buckeyes for the rest of our lives."

Okay, that should have been the end of it.

But Justin Boren, even though he had to sit out the 2008 season due to NCAA transfer rules, quickly turned into the tool that most OSU players become. He was photographed at a Halloween party at OSU that October…dressed as Michigan coach Rich Rodriguez.

Wow. Just, wow. Guess it's true—as soon as you step on that campus, you become an imbecile.

CHRIS SPIELMAN

It's hard to hate Chris Spielman. Hard. But not impossible. After all, check out these quotes from last year during a radio interview. Once a Buckeye, always a Buckeye, partiality be damned:

> Now their defense on the other hand, it is the worst Michigan defense ever in the history of Michigan football in my opinion. They are so bad. They can't tackle. In my way of thinking, I don't know how they got this bad on defense.

OHIO STATE

OSU PLAYERS CURRENTLY IN THE NFL

PLAYER	TEAM	POSITION
Allen, Will	Pittsburgh Steelers	Safety
Ballard, Jake	New York Giants	Tight End
Boone, Alex	San Francisco 49ers	Off. Tackle
Carpenter, Bobby	Detroit Lions	Linebacker
Clements, Nate	San Francisco 49ers	Cornerback
Coleman, Kurt	Philadelphia Eagles	Safety
Cordle, Jim	New York Giants	Center
Diggs, Na'il	St. Louis Rams	Linebacker
Gamble, Chris	Carolina Panthers	Cornerback
Gholston, Vernon	New York Jets	Defensive End
Gibson, Thaddeus	San Francisco 49ers	Linebacker
Ginn, Ted	San Francisco 49ers	Wide Receiver
Gonzalez, Anthony	Indianapolis Colts	Wide Receiver
Grant, Larry	St. Louis Rams	Linebacker
Hartline, Brian	Miami Dolphins	Wide Receiver
Hawk, A.J.	Green Bay Packers	Linebacker
Holmes, Santonio	New York Jets	Wide Receiver
Houser, Kevin	Baltimore Ravens	Long Snapper
Jenkins, Malcolm	New Orleans Saints	Cornerback
Jenkins, Michael	Atlanta Falcons	Wide Receiver
Laurinaitis, James	St. Louis Rams	Linebacker
Mangold, Nick	New York Jets	Center
Nickey, Donnie	Tennessee Titans	Safety
Nugent, Mike	Cincinnati Bengals	Place-kicker
Pickett, Ryan	Green Bay Packers	Def. Tackle
Richardson, Jay	Seattle Seahawks	Defensive End

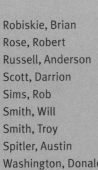

Robiskie, Brian	Cleveland Browns	Wide Receiver
Rose, Robert	Miami Dolphins	Defensive End
Russell, Anderson	Washington Redskins	Safety
Scott, Darrion	Washington Redskins	Defensive End
Sims, Rob	Detroit Lions	Guard
Smith, Will	New Orleans Saints	Defensive End
Smith, Troy	San Francisco 49ers	Quarterback
Spitler, Austin	Miami Dolphins	Linebacker
Washington, Donald	Kansas City Chiefs	Cornerback
Wells, Beanie	Arizona Cardinals	Running Back
Whitner, Donte	Buffalo Bills	Safety
Wilhelm, Matt	Green Bay Packers	Linebacker
Winfield, Antoine	Minnesota Vikings	Cornerback
Worthington, Doug	Tampa Bay Buccaneers	Defensive End
Youboty, Ashton	Buffalo Bills	Cornerback

OHIO STATE

You look at Ohio State, when they lose players, we've had injuries, has this defense taken a noticeable step back? No. It still maintains. It still goes. Everybody is saying, "Well, they're all young, they're all coming back." Well, yeah, they're all coming back. It's on the worst defense in the NCAA they're all coming back. Is that so exciting for you? It's bad. [Nose tackle Mike] Martin is the only guy that could start at Ohio State—the only guy that could start. He would roll in there. He's a good player. But other than that, these guys would be excellent special teams guys. Very good on special teams.... It's a combination of poor recruiting, in my opinion, I think Coach Carr [who retired after the 2007 season], to be perfectly honest, left the cupboard bare in his last few years. I don't think they recruited the talent, because you look at the upperclassmen that they have. They're all great kids. I had a chance to meet with a bunch of them. They practice hard, they play hard, and they're tough, but it comes down to one thing when you're talking about playing at a high level like Michigan is used to playing at, and that's talent. And they have zero on defense. One kid, the Martin kid. Other than that, a lot of guys would be nice little subs at Indiana.

Ouch. Hey, Chris, tell us how you really feel.

Still, the hatred for Spielman is minimal, at best. He's actually one of the good guys, and he has a Michigan connection. After Spielman left Ohio State as a two-time All-American and the 1987 Lombardi Trophy winner, he was the heart and soul and anchor of some pretty bad Detroit Lions teams. He played 10 seasons in the NFL for the Lions and Buffalo Bills. His 1,138 career tackles at Detroit was a team record, and he played in four Pro Bowls. Upon his retirement, he began a broadcasting career with FOX Sports and ESPN.

Spielman's decision to take a year off from football while playing with the Bills to be with his wife, Stefanie, touched many hearts. Stefanie fought a 12-year battle with breast cancer before passing away in November of 2009.

GOMER JONES

Gomer Jones was the star of the Ohio State football teams from 1933 through 1935, playing center on offense and linebacker on defense. He was the team captain in 1935 and a consensus All-American. He was the 15th player selected in the 1936 NFL Draft but opted to pursue a coaching career instead. He was an assistant at Oklahoma for 17 years under Bud Wilkinson. The Sooners won national championships in 1950, '55, and '56, and set an NCAA record with 47 consecutive wins. When Wilkinson retired in 1964, Jones was named Oklahoma's head coach. His teams were 9–11–1 in two seasons. Jones resigned as head coach, but became the school's athletics director, a position he held until his death in 1971. He was inducted into the College Football Hall of Fame in 1978.

Why do we hate him?

We really don't. We just think his name is perfectly symbolic for the Ohio State football program. They're a bunch of Gomers.

JIM OTIS

Jim Otis came to Ohio State via a bit of nepotism. His father, James John Otis, was roommates with none other than Woodrow Hayes when both were members of the Sigma Chi fraternity at Denison University. Thus, Jim's matriculation to Ohio State was somewhat preordained.

Otis led the Buckeyes in rushing from 1967 to 1969. He helped lead the Buckeyes to an undefeated season in 1968 and was a first-team All-America fullback in '69. He remains second (to Archie Griffin) on Ohio State's career rushing-yards-per game list. He played nine years in the NFL. His best season was 1975, when he rushed for 1,076 yards with the St. Louis Cardinals and was selected for the Pro Bowl.

What's not to like? Well, here's one thing—legend has it that Otis begged back into the 1968 Michigan–Ohio State game late in the fourth quarter when the Buckeyes were driving for another touchdown. Otis scored, giving him four TDs on the day, and OSU rolled up the score to the 50–14 final in the game where Hayes went for two-points despite being up by 36 points.

Kind of a dick move by Otis but, you know, what do you expect from a Buckeye?

3

TRADITIONS WE HATE

TRADITIONS ARE WHAT MAKE COLLEGE FOOTBALL special. Traditions are what make college football unique.

There's Howard's Rock at Clemson, Georgia's bulldog UGA, the Sooner Schooner at Oklahoma, cowbells at Mississippi State, the 12th man at Texas A&M, all the great traditions at the University of Michigan…we could go on and on. But the more we go on, it still won't include the so-called traditions at Ohio State. Frankly, they're just not good enough to be included in the pantheon of *great* traditions.

THE OHIO STATE MARCHING BAND AND SCRIPT OHIO

The public address announcer at Ohio Stadium intones before every game, "And now, the most memorable tradition in college band history, the incomparable Script Ohio!"

Memorable? Incomparable? Hardly.

As we've noted elsewhere in this book, there are fatal flaws in the OSU marching band calling itself The Best Damn Band in the Land, or TBDBITL for short, and for claiming that the

A tolerable college band spells out "Ohio" in script, a trick they learned from the University of Michigan Marching Band. Photo courtesy of Getty Images

script "Ohio" it forms on the football field at Ohio Stadium is the most memorable tradition in college football.

The flaws are as follows: It's not the best damn band in the land, not by a long shot. It's not the most memorable tradition in college football, not by a long shot.

Listen, it's a nice little maneuver. And the band is tolerable. Any exercise in hyperbole beyond that only feeds into the braggadocio mentality that OSU feels it must use to stroke its ego—among other things—about feeling like a second-class citizen when compared to Michigan.

Truth be told, there would be no Script Ohio if it wasn't for the University of Michigan. True story. In the immortal words of Senator Bob Dole, I know it, you know it, and the American people know it.

And so does Ohio State.

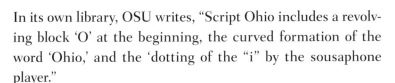

In its own library, OSU writes, "Script Ohio includes a revolving block 'O' at the beginning, the curved formation of the word 'Ohio,' and the 'dotting of the "i" by the sousaphone player."

But where did the inspiration come from? According to the OSU Marching Band's history, band director Eugene Weigel said, "Searching for ideas, I remembered the rotating sign around the Times Square Building in New York City, during my student days at Columbus, and also the sky-writing advertisements at state fair time." However, Weigel was also present in 1932 when the University of Michigan Marching Band took the field at Ohio Stadium. According to the student newspaper, *Michigan Daily*, "Probably the most effective single formation was the word 'Ohio' spelled out in script diagonally across the field in the double-deck Ohio stadium to the accompaniment of the OSU marching song, 'Fight the Team.'" Other Michigan band formations were "Mich," a block "O," and a block "M."

Ted Boehm, OSU marching band member in 1935 and 1936, and considered an "authority" on Script Ohio, wrote that indeed, Michigan had performed the first Ohio in script. The University of Illinois' marching band also performed a script Ohio at the OSU game in 1936, after the OSU band had already done one, with a number of musicians dotting the "i." But are the scripts equivalent to the OSU Script Ohio? Boehm wrote: "We submit that the script aspect is only one part of the overall event that is signified by the name. Of course, the script is the one essential element, but there is more; all of the parts have merged, starting with the triple revolving block Ohio as the lead-off formation, the peel-off into the script movement, the interlaced shoestring movement, the pervasive driving beat of the venerable 'Le Regiment de Sambre et Meuse,' the dotted 'i' and the concluding vocal chorus."

Okay, that's what's known as "splitting hairs." First, the tacit admission that Script Ohio actually came from Michigan, but then a quick, "Oh, but we dot the 'i' and we form it out of a block 'O' so this is the true version."

Riiiiiiight. Pull this other leg and it plays "Jingle Bells"…again.

As noted, the Script Ohio is done to "Le Regiment de Sambre et Meuse," a military march from France. Translated, it means, "We French put our tails between our legs and run at the first sign of confrontation, and so does the Ohio State football team."

Now, as for the band. The Best Damn Band in the Land? Well, it's certainly top five. Good? Yes. Best? No. I'd say the rankings go like this: No. 5, Ohio State Marching Band; No. 4, Massachusetts' Minutemen Marching Band; No. 3, Purdue's All-American Marching Band; No. 2, Texas' Longhorn Band; and No. 1, University of Michigan Marching Band.

By the way, that's the name of the band—the University of Michigan Marching Band. Nothing else. No self-congratulatory pat on the back to proclaim ourselves as the best damn band in the land. No need to say it; everybody already knows it.

Even the acronym is foolish. TBDBITL? Sorry, it doesn't roll off the tongue—like, say, NORAD or J-Lo, or A-Rod—and it's even more ridiculous to write it. Then again, perhaps it stands for: This. Band. Doesn't. Belong. In. The. Least.

Or maybe it's: The. Biggest. Dumbest. Band. In. The. Land.

Whatever. Bottom line is, they're a good band, not the best. They'd give the local elementary school band a run for their money, that's for sure.

"HANG ON SLOOPY"

Apparently, one of the big deals for the Ohio State Marching Band is to play the 1960s hit "Hang On Sloopy" at every event it attends. As usual, there's a stupid backstory to the whole thing.

The McCoys, who recorded the song in 1965, were originally from Dayton, Ohio. The song was about Dorothy Sloop of Steubenville, Ohio, a singer who sometimes performed under the name "Sloopy." That same year, John Tatgenhorst, a member of the OSU band, wrote his own arrangement for the song and convinced Dr. Charles Spohn, then the band director, to allow the band to play it at a game. On October 9, 1965, "Hang On Sloopy" was played during a rainy contest against Illinois. The initial impression wasn't too good, but it slowly caught on with the simple-minded OSU fans.

According to the band's Web site, tbdbitl.osu.edu, "The ability of the song to bring the crowd to its feet has been noted by university officials, particularly in the press box. During the OSU vs. Syracuse game in 1988, Dr. Jon Woods was asked not to play 'Sloopy' again until they had time to structurally test

OHIO STATE

A MASCOT? REALLY? *REALLY?*

The University of Michigan football team doesn't have a mascot, and we don't need no stinkin' mascot. Especially in light of...this:

Um, what the hell is *that*? Ostensibly, it's supposed to be a nut—a Buckeye nut—come to life. Brutus Buckeye, to be exact.

No more needs to be said. This entire book could be filled with adjectives to describe how utterly ridiculous and embarrassing this mascot is. Seriously, Woody let them get away with this when it was introduced back in 1965?!?

the press box. Evidently, there were reports that the press box was shaking. Dr. Paul Droste confirms this rhythmic power, noting that 'Sloopy' was used on several occasions to test the structural integrity of the stadium."

Okay, as a longtime sportswriter, I'm calling BS on that one. The press box was rocking? The press box never rocks. Oh, you'll get your occasional homer in there wearing his Ohio State jersey and cheering on the team, showing not one iota of press box etiquette and breaking cardinal rule No. 1—No Cheering in the Press Box. But I highly doubt that a bunch of sportswriters were getting up and shakin' it to "Hang On Sloopy" enough to make the press box structurally unsound. Unless, you know, it was built by an Ohio architect and engineer. Then I could see if it had problems.

So, moving on. In 1985, 20 years after "Hang On Sloopy" was first played at Ohio State games, a columnist for the former *Columbus Citizen-Journal* wrote a piece about the State of Washington considering the adoption of its own rock song. In its infinite wisdom, the Ohio State General Assembly couldn't find anything better to do, so it quickly responded by making "Hang On Sloopy" the official rock song of the state of Ohio.

No, actually, I'm not kidding. Here's the resolution, with, um, a few comments from your intrepid author in italics.

> HOUSE CONCURRENT RESOLUTION NO. 16
>   WHEREAS, The members of the 116th General Assembly of Ohio wish to recognize the rock song "Hang On Sloopy" as the official rock song of the great State of Ohio; and

WHEREAS, In 1965, an Ohio-based rock group known as the McCoys reached the top of the national record charts with "Hang On Sloopy," (*Okay, it was top of the charts for one week, according to Billboard, from October 2 to October 9, and it was the group's only No. 1 hit*) composed by Bert Russell and Wes Farrell, and that same year, John Tatgenhorst, then an arranger for the Ohio State University Marching Band, created the band's now-famous arrangement of "Sloopy," first performed at the Ohio State–Illinois football game on October 9, 1965; and

WHEREAS, Rock music has become an integral part of American culture, having attained a degree of acceptance no one would have thought possible twenty years ago; (*Really? No one thought possible that rock music was accepted in 1965, which was almost 10 years after Elvis Presley and a year after The Beatles stormed America?*); and

WHEREAS, Adoption of "Hang On Sloopy" as the official rock song of Ohio is in no way intended to supplant "Beautiful Ohio" as the official state song, (*nothing is as oxymoronic as "Beautiful Ohio"*) but would serve as a companion piece to that old chestnut; and

WHEREAS, If fans of jazz, country-and-western, classical, Hawaiian and polka music (*because nothing says "Ohio State" like the "I'm Gonna Get a Dummy" polka by Frank Yankovic*) think those styles also should be recognized by the state, then by golly, they can push their own resolution just like we're doing; and

WHEREAS, "Hang On Sloopy" is of particular relevance to members of the Baby Boom Generation (*relevance? A one-hit wonder?*), who were once dismissed as a bunch of long-haired, crazy kids, but who now are old enough and vote in sufficient numbers to be taken quite seriously; and

WHEREAS, Adoption of this resolution will not take too long, cost the state anything, or affect the quality of life in this state to any appreciable degree, and if we in the legislature just go ahead and pass the darn thing, we can get on with more important stuff (*yeah, like Warren Harding and the Ohio Gang, Coingate, Wayne Hays and Elizabeth Ray, etc.*); and

WHEREAS, Sloopy lives in a very bad part of town (*it's based on a chick from Steubenville, what do you expect?*), and everybody, yeah, tries to put my Sloopy down; and

WHEREAS, Sloopy, I don't care what your daddy do, 'cause you know, Sloopy girl, I'm in love with you (*ah, I see what you were doing there, quoting the lyrics…very sly!*); therefore be it Resolved, That we, the members of the 116th General Assembly of Ohio, in adopting this Resolution, name "Hang On Sloopy" as the official rock song of the State of Ohio; and be it further Resolved, That the Legislative Clerk of the House of Representatives transmit duly authenticated copies of this Resolution to the news media of Ohio. (*Yes, because we're sure it was the biggest news story of the day.*)

Now, far be it from us to influence opinion. So, judge for yourself. Here are the lyrics to "Hang On Sloopy." Keeper? Or vote it off the island?

Hang on Sloopy, Sloopy, hang on
Hang on Sloopy, Sloopy hang on

Sloopy lives in a very bad part of town
and everybody, yeah, tries to put my Sloopy down
Sloopy I don't care, what your daddy do

Cuz you know Sloopy, girl, I'm in love with you
and so I sing out

Hang on Sloopy, Sloopy hang on
Hang on Sloopy, Sloopy hang on

Sloopy wears a red dress, yeah
As old as the hills
but when Sloopy wears that red dress, yeah
you know it gives me the chills

Sloopy when I see you walking,
walking down the street
I say don't worry Sloopy, girl
You belong to me
and so I sing out

Hang on Sloopy, Sloopy hang on
Hang on Sloopy, Sloopy hang on
(yeah) (yeah) (yeah) (yeah) Let's give it to 'em
(Guitar solo)

Sloopy let your hair down, girl
Let it hang down on me
Sloopy let your hair down, girl
Let it hang down on me, yeah

Come on Sloopy (come on, come on)
Oh come on Sloopy (come on, come on)
Oh come on Sloopy (come on, come on)
Oh come on Sloopy (come on, come on)

Well it feels so good (come on, come on)
You know it feels so good (come on, come on)
Well shake it, shake it, shake it Sloopy (come on, come on)
Shake it, shake it, shake it yeah (come on, come on)
(Scream)

Hang on Sloopy, Sloopy hang on
(yeah) (yeah) (yeah) (yeah)
Hang on Sloopy, Sloopy hang on
(yeah) (yeah) (yeah) (yeah)
Hang on Sloopy, Sloopy hang on

BUCKEYES BOOKS WE HATE

1968: THE YEAR THAT SAVED OHIO STATE FOOTBALL, David Hyde

I REMEMBER WOODY, Steve Greenberg and Dale Ratermann (*the guy was such a jerk he needed two authors to tell his story*)

GREATEST MOMENTS IN OHIO STATE FOOTBALL HISTORY, Bruce Hooley (*do they really have enough to fill a book? Probably a picture pop-up book*)

THE WINNERS MANUAL: FOR THE GAME OF LIFE, Jim Tressel (*who?*)

A FIRE TO WIN: THE LIFE AND TIMES OF WOODY HAYES, John Lombardo

There's a lot of "yeah-yeahs" in there, don't you think? Now, if it were me, and I'm this dude from the band back in the mid-'60s, and I'm looking to have a little fun and eventually create a signature song, I go a completely different route. Here are 20 songs from 1964 through 1966 that I would put waaaaay before "Hang On Sloopy."

"Can't Buy Me Love" (The Beatles)
"I Get Around" (The Beach Boys)
"Do Wah Diddy Diddy" (Manfred Mann)
"Leader of the Pack" (The Shangri-Las)
"Come See About Me" (The Supremes)
"Stop! In the Name of Love" (The Supremes)
"Ticket To Ride" (The Beatles)
"Help Me Rhonda" (The Beach Boys)
"I Can't Help Myself" (The Four Tops)
"Satisfaction" (The Rolling Stones)
"Help! " (The Beatles)
"Eve of Destruction" (Barry McGuire)
"Get Off of My Cloud" (The Rolling Stones)
"Over and Over" (The Dave Clark Five)
"These Boots Are Made for Walkin'" (Nancy Sinatra)
"Good Lovin'" (The Young Rascals)
"Paint it Black" (The Rolling Stones)
"Hanky Panky" (Tommy James and the Shondells)
"Wild Thing" (The Troggs)
"I'm a Believer" (The Monkees)

BUCKEYE GROVE

This is a good one. You break your back, maybe even literally. You work your tail off, you give maximum effort even in practices, you're a natural leader, and you absolutely own your position. You are the preeminent player, the master of your domain. You become a college football All-American, an honor among the highest in any sport.

And at Ohio State, what do you get for your efforts? A tree.

No, seriously. A tree.

Buckeye Grove runs along Ohio Stadium. Any time an OSU player earns first-team All-America status, a tree is planted in his name, along with a plaque. The tradition started in 1934, although players who attained All-America status prior to that have been honored. From Boyd Cherry in 1914 to James Laurinaitis and Malcolm Jenkins in 2008, there have been 130 players named All-America at Ohio State.

Plantings and ceremonies are conducted each spring prior to the spring game.

"THE BUCKEYE BATTLE CRY"

Okay, this is not "The Victors." It's not "On Wisconsin," it's not "Onward to Victory," it's not the "Notre Dame Victory March," it's not even the "Marist College Fight Song."

"The Buckeye Battle Cry" is devoid of even the slightest trace of rah-rah spirit. It's a disjointed musical arrangement, and even the words are a bunch of mumbo-jumbo. You know what a goose-bump-inducing, spine-tingling event it is to hear 110,000 people sing "The Victors" at Michigan Stadium? Now imagine 105,000 singing "The Buckeye Battle Cry" at Ohio Stadium. Right. It's like listening to William Hung.

In old Ohio there's a team
That's known throughout the land
Eleven warriors brave and bold
Whose fame will ever stand
And when the ball goes over,
Our cheers will reach the sky
Ohio Field will hear again
The Buckeye Battle Cry!

Drive, drive on down the field
Men of the Scarlet and Gray
Don't let them through that line
We've got to win this game today
COME ON OHIO!

Smash through to victory
We cheer you as you go
Our honor defend
We will fight to the end
for O-HI-O!

Yup. She bang.

BUCKEYE LEAVES

Ohio State's nickname is based on a nut. Doesn't that just say it all?

But beginning in 1967, the school took the tradition further and began awarding those little marijuana plant stickers you see on players' helmets, otherwise known as Buckeye Leaves. The first sticker that then-coach Woody Hayes awarded was to

Michigan Men perform to the best of their abilites to further the team and win games. Ohio State players like to make their coaches happy so they can get a sticker.

Jim Nein, for an interception against Oregon in a 30–0 victory. A year later, the practice was enhanced as Hayes and trainer Ernie Biggs began giving players helmet stickers resembling buckeye leaves for outstanding performances in games.

And what constitutes an outstanding performance? Glad you asked. I could provide you a list of the individual and team achievements that each player gets rewarded for, but it would take a complicated chart and another three pages of patience to wade through (trust me on this). There are percentages of goals (a tailback who performs 90 percent of his film grade standard as set by the staff receives a leaf), certain unit designations (a defensive unit that had five "three and outs" gets a leaf), and basic criteria (everyone gets a leaf for a win).

The point is: the Ohio State program is incentive-laden and individualistic. It has to bribe its players to get them to perform. At Michigan, we just go out and play the game as hard as we can. The reward is winning.

THE VICTORY BELL

The Victory Bell tradition began on October 2, 1954, after a victory against Cal. Located in the southeast corner of Ohio Stadium, the victory bell is rung for 15 minutes after a victory—but for 30 minutes after a win over Michigan.

THE GOLD PANTS

In 1934, when Francis Schmidt took over as head coach of the Ohio State football program, he was asked how he would beat Michigan, which at the time had a fairly sizeable victory advantage over the Buckeyes. Schmidt replied with a rather long-winded answer that ended with the now-famous quote, "They put their pants on one leg at a time, same as we do."

And thus was the basis for the Gold Pants Club, which Schmidt helped put together. Every time the Buckeyes beat the Wolverines, each member of the OSU program receives a gold charm resembling Michigan's maize pants. Why it isn't called the Maize Pants Club, we have no idea. They're Ohioans, whaddya want?

Anyhoo, this is just another of the many ridiculous Ohio State "traditions." I mean, seriously, the thing looks like a tooth.

4
COACHES WE HATE

THIS SECTION COULD FILL A BOOK. A whole book.

And on just two men, to boot. Ironically, the one who was arguably the meanest man in college football and the one who just had to resign are the two winningest coaches in the program. That says something right there.

The debacle that was Jim Tressel has already been covered in the introduction to this side of the book. You do things as deplorable as Tressel, you get moved to the front of the line. How he cheated and why he cheated could (and probably will) fill volumes. We'll leave all that to the introduction for now. As for Woody and more on Tressel, we'll get to them in a moment.

First, the appetizers.

JOHN WILCE

Ohio State has had 22 head coaches in its painfully long and inglorious history, and Wilce was just one of four (Hayes, John Cooper, and Tressel being the other three) to coach 10 years or longer.

Wilce was in charge from 1913 to 1928, and is thought of as OSU's first coaching "star." He helped usher Ohio State football into the national picture by coaching the team to three conference titles, as well as mentoring 15 All-Americans, including the school's first, Boyd Cherry, and the player generally considered the Buckeyes' first real standout, Chic Harley.

Wilce was also in charge for two momentous occasions—when the school joined the Western Conference, which was later to become the Big Ten, and when Ohio Stadium debuted in 1922. Interestingly, Wilce resigned from his coaching career at Ohio State to become a physician; he later taught at the school.

FRANCIS SCHMIDT

We've covered the Schmidt saga before. He took over the program in 1934 and uttered the famous "They put their pants on one leg at a time same as everybody else" comment in reference to Michigan, leading to the creation of one of the dumbest traditions in college football, the Gold Pants Club.

Schmidt played football at the University of Nebraska. Following law school at Nebraska and a stint in the Army, Schmidt began his head coaching career. He was head coach at Tulsa (1919–1921), Arkansas (1922–1928), and Texas Christian (1929–1933). In 1934 Schmidt was named the head coach at Ohio State. His initial Buckeyes team went 7–1, including a 5–1 mark in the Big Ten. The following season, the Buckeyes were 5–0 in the conference and 7–1 overall. In seven years,

Ohio State head football coach Francis A. Schmidt, pictured in 1934, was clever enough to tell his players how to get dressed. His "They put their pants on one leg at a time same as everybody else" cliché morphed into another dumb OSU tradition: the Gold Pants Club.

Ohio State was 39–16–1 overall and 30–9–1 in the conference, including two titles.

EARLE BRUCE

Give him credit for this—Earle Bruce was Ohio State through and through. A knee injury in 1951 cut short his OSU playing career, and he was so devastated that he left school and returned home, only to be summoned back to Columbus by

Earl Bruce is lifted up on the shoulders of his players after leading Ohio State past Michigan 23–20 in Ann Arbor on November 21, 1987, just days after he was fired.

first-year coach Woody Hayes to join the coaching staff as a student assistant.

Following his graduation from Ohio State in 1953, Bruce started on a phenomenal high school coaching career, posting an 82–12–3 record at Salem, Sandusky, and then famed Massillon High during a 10-year career. Bruce briefly returned to OSU as a Hayes assistant for one year before taking the head job at the University of Tampa, where a 10–2 mark and a victory in the Tangerine Bowl landed him the head job at Iowa State. He stayed in Ames for six seasons, from 1973 to 1978, compiling a 36–32 record and two bowl game appearances.

That, apparently, was enough for him to return to Ohio State as the head coach after Hayes graduated from slugging his own players behind closed doors to hitting opposing players on national television.

Bruce's first team in 1979 finished 8–0 in the Big Ten and 11–1 overall, the only loss coming in the Rose Bowl. But then came six consecutive seasons of 9–3, a 10–3 mark in 1986, and then a 6–4–1 disaster in 1987. He was fired the week before the Michigan game. All told, Bruce went 81–26–1 overall, 57–17 in the Big Ten, won or shared four Big Ten championships, had a winning record in bowl games (5–3), and had a winning record against Michigan.

Yet, unlike John Cooper, Bruce is a welcome sight back on the Columbus campus. He is an analyst for Buckeyes games and a frequent speaker on the charity circuit.

PAUL BROWN

Paul Brown has a bit of a checkered history with Ohio State. According to OhioHistoryCentral.org, Brown was a highly successful coach at Washington High School in Massillon, Ohio, compiling a record of 80–8–2 over eight seasons. Due to his stellar high school coaching record, Ohio State appointed Brown as the school's football coach in 1941. He coached just four seasons, but he went 18–8–1 and in 1942 led the Buckeyes to their first-ever national championship.

OHIO STATE

OHIO STATE COACHING RECORDS

Coach	Years	vs.U-M	Overall
Alexander S. Lilley	1890–1891	0–0	3–5
Jack Ryder	1892–1895		
	1898	0–0	22–22–2
Charles Hickey	1896	0–0	5–5–1
David F. Edwards	1897	0–1	1–7–1
John B. Eckstorm	1899–1901	0–1–1	22–4–3
Perry Hale	1902–1903	0–2	14–5–2
E.R. Sweatland	1903–1905	0–2	14–7–2
Albert H. Hernstein	1906–1909	0–4	28–10–1
Howard Jones	1910	0–0–1	6–1–3
Henry Vaughn	1911	0–1	5–3–2
John R. Richards	1912	0–1	6–3
John W. Wilce	1913–1928	4–7	78–33–9
Sam S. Willaman	1929–1932	2–3	26–10–5
Francis A. Schmidt	1934–1940	4–3	39–16–1
Paul E. Brown	1940–1943	1–1–1	18–8–1
Carroll C. Widdoes	1944–1945	1–1	16–2
Paul O. Bixlar	1946	0–1	4–3–2
Wesley E. Fesler	1947–1950	0–3–1	21–13–3
Woody Hayes	1951–1978	16–11–1	205–61–10
Earle Bruce	1979–1987	5–4	81–26–1
John Cooper	1988–2000	2–10–1	111–43–4
Jim Tressel	2001–2010	9–1	105–22

Brown was inducted into the U.S. Navy in 1944. While serving, he was head coach of the Great Lakes Naval Station football team. His Bluejackets squad went 15–5–2 in two years. Following the war, like many of his former players, Brown didn't return to Columbus. He opted to take a position with the new Cleveland team in the All-America Football Conference as part-owner, vice president, general manager, and head coach. So popular was Brown that in a poll of the team's fans, the nickname "Browns" was selected, and thus was born the Cleveland Browns.

The Browns organization won the AAFC championship the four seasons that it played in the league.

With Brown as coach, the Browns won three NFL titles (1950, 1954, and 1955). Brown remained as the team's head coach until 1962, when a new owner, Art Modell, fired the only coach the team had known in 17 years of existence. It wouldn't be Modell's first run-in with Cleveland fans—in 1996 he effectively moved the franchise to Baltimore in an agreement with the NFL. The city of Cleveland retained the "Browns" name, and it was announced that a new Cleveland Browns franchise would return to the city in three years. Modell moved the Browns east to Baltimore, and the team became the Ravens, going on to win the 2001 Super Bowl against the New York Giants.

Brown, meanwhile, resurfaced in Cincinnati, where he coached the Bengals from 1968 to 1975. All told, he finished his pro coaching career with a record of 206–104–10, with seven league titles in 25 seasons. His coaching tree is impeccable—among the coaches who either played for him or coached under him were Don Shula, Bill Walsh, Lou Saban, Weeb Ewbank, Otto Graham, Chuck Noll, Ara Parseghian, Blanton Collier, Sid Gillman, Abe Gibron, Bruce Coslet, and Sam Wyche. (The hate comes from the fact that Don Shula coached the Dolphins, and we're Jets fans, and Bruce Coslet eventually coached the Jets. Enough said.)

An ironic part of this whole story is that Brown's successful coaching career in the pros might have been cut short had he gotten his wish and returned to Ohio State. When the school was looking for a coach to replace Wes Fesler in 1951, Brown was interested in the job. But he had pissed off many of the Buckeyes faithful when he did not return to Columbus following World War II, and also for signing many Ohio State players to professional contracts before their college eligibility had expired (though the practice was allowed at the time). He did have an official job interview with school officials, but the University Board rejected Brown and instead chose a man by the name of Woody Hayes.

WOODY HAYES

Woody Hayes was a mean, vile man. Ohio State fans will try to spin you on that and say he was a disciplinarian who practiced tough love. No, that was Bo Schembechler. Hayes was just a mean, crochety old man even when he wasn't an old man. Worse, Ohio State fans also go into a deep spin—read: it was justified and it was "only" one time— over the Charlie Bauman incident, in which Hayes punched the Clemson player in the 1978 Gator Bowl and was fired over the incident.

Wayne Woodrow Hayes was born—get this—on Valentine's Day, 1913. He is a native Ohioan, born in Clifton and raised in Newcomerstown. He attended Denison University in Granville, Ohio, where he played football. After graduating in 1935 with a B.A. in English and history, Hayes became an assistant coach at Mingo Junction High School in Ohio that fall. He remained there for two seasons before moving to New Philadelphia High School, also in Ohio, as an assistant coach. In 1938 Hayes was promoted to head coach at New Philadelphia. Three years later, he enlisted in the United States Navy, where he developed a passion for military history, according to a well-written biography on vegasbettinglines.com.

Hayes saw combat duty in the Pacific and finished his tour as a lieutenant commander in 1946. He returned to his alma mater and coached at Denison for three seasons, including back-to-back undefeated seasons (9–0 and 8–0) in 1947 and 1948. At the age of 36, he became head coach at Miami of Ohio, actually starting something of a tradition at the school known as the Cradle of Coaches.

The team went 5–4 in his first year in 1949, then went 9–1, including a bowl game victory over Arizona State, in 1950. That was it for Hayes at Miami. He was hired by Ohio State and began his career with the Buckeyes in 1951, saying famously, "I'm not coming here looking for security. I came here for the opportunity."

In his first year the Buckeyes had trouble adapting to the T formation that Hayes preferred and finished with a 4–3–2 record. The next season, however, Ohio State improved to

From before he was hired by the Buckeyes in 1951 to after he was fired for punching an opposing player in 1978, Woody Hayes was outrageous, ridiculous, and just plain mean.

6–3. More important, the team snapped an eight-year losing streak against Michigan, a victory that immediately endeared Hayes to Buckeyes fans.

The rest, of course, is history. Hayes adopted the three-yards-and-a-cloud-of-dust philosophy, famously noting, "There are three things that can happen when you pass, and two of them ain't good."

Hayes won three national championships at Ohio State during his career, 13 Big Ten championships, and in 28 years was 16–11–1 against Michigan. Unfortunately, all his great work both on and off the field remains mired behind his volatile temper, his outrageous personality, generally mean persona, ridiculous quotes, and, finally, the Charlie Bauman incident.

In the counterpart to this book, the Ohio State enthusiasts write about their favorite story involving Hayes. In 1974 Hayes brought his undefeated, No. 1–ranked team to Michigan State, and the Buckeyes were upset 16–13—but not before fullback Champ Henson had scored what appeared to be the winning touchdown in the final moments of the game, only to have the referees say he didn't break the plane of the goal line. In the OSU locker room, Hayes went berserk, of course. Reminded by several people to calm down—he had a heart attack a year earlier—Hayes apparently took his heart medicine, threw it on the floor, and stepped on it, shouting, "Fuck my heart!" He then turned to his team and said, "You motherfuckers like to fight, don't you? Let's go kick their asses." The players lined up behind Hayes, who then ran into then–Big Ten commissioner Wayne Duke as he stepped out of the locker room. Hayes confronted Duke and said, "Tell my team they got fucked." Duke said, "Woody, they got fucked." Hayes then backed down and told his team to get on the bus. As they left the stadium, a group of Spartans' fans stood in front of the bus, heckling the Buckeyes. Hayes told the driver, "Fuck 'em. Run 'em over." The bus was able to leave the stadium without further incident.

The sad part about this whole story, of course, is that if Hayes had not been confronted by Duke, if the Michigan State students had not backed down, he would have led the Buckeyes into a fight and would have had the driver start to drive toward the students.

Much has been made of Hayes' philosophies and wisdom. Here are a plethora of quotes from the man himself that paint an ironic picture of Hayes. For every compelling quote, there's a mean-spirited or idiotic one.

Woody on Ohio State

"I feel sometimes that the man upstairs sort of likes us. Maybe He was testing us, saying, 'Let's see what kind of people are at Ohio State. Do they take defeat lightly? Can they come back from adversity?'"

"Our kind of families win a few more football games than others."

"We make no apologies for winning or for aiming our entire program toward that goal."

"You're from Ohio and you belong at Ohio State." —to Champ Henson

"If we worked half as hard as our band, we'd be champions."

"Who is the greatest track man in history? Why, it's Jesse Owens! He won so many gold medals that Hitler left the stadium in Berlin because he didn't want to recognize that this great athlete from Ohio State was superior. And who is the greatest college football player? Why, it's Arch [Archie Griffin]. Nobody else in the history of football has ever won two Heisman trophies. And who is the greatest golfer of all time? Why, it's Jack Nicklaus. Nobody can touch him. He's the best. And who is the greatest in basketball? Why, it's John Havlicek. He's Mr. Basketball."

"Now that's enough of that! To hell with Notre Dame. Let's talk about *our own* university." —to Paul Hornung and a professor discussing Notre Dame football

"Unbiased, hell. We're Ohio State guys and don't you ever forget it." —to a broadcast partner who praised a Michigan play

"Some people accuse me of buying football players at Ohio State. Hell, I don't buy football players. I sell 'em!"

"No, goddamnit, you bastards are going to have to fire me." —to athletics director Hugh Hindman and Ohio State President Harold Enarson after the Bauman incident at the Gator Bowl

"You will win on Saturday. You will have to do what we have planned to do all week, but essentially you will win because you are Ohio State, and they will respect you for that. They know what we do, and they will respect you. And I'll tell you something else! That respect soon turns to fear, and by the time we've hit them three or four times in that first quarter, they know they can't win."

Woody on Football
"Perfect preparation prevents piss-poor performance."

"You're overofficiating the offense and letting the defense get away with murder. The Bible says turn the other cheek, but I'll be damned if I'll tell my kids to do that when they'll just get it fractured." —to officials in a 1960 game

"Sherman ran an option play right through the South."

"Somebody asked me the other day what all these so-called critics wanted, and I said, 'I know what they want. They want to destroy college football.' Well, dammit all, they're not going to destroy a very wonderful American institution."

"I will pound you and pound you until you quit."

"The only fun about being here is winning the game." —on the 1974 Rose Bowl

"Winning takes care of everything."

"There will be no practice on Friday. By that time, the hay is in the barn."

"Football polls are a joke."

"Pride is a great asset. No real football player should be without it."

"We allot four seats to each faculty member, and that's too damned many."

"A bunch of crooks." —describing referees from the 1971 Michigan game

MORE BUCKEYES QUOTES WE HATE

"Because I couldn't go for three." —surly, vindictive OSU coach Woody Hayes on why he went for a two-point conversation late in the 1968 game, a 50–14 Ohio State victory. He got his the next year when U-M upset what he called his greatest team ever.

"I play against better defensive backs than [Charles Woodson] in practice every day." —Buckeyes receiver David Boston prior to the 1997 game. Boston caught a TD pass in the game, but Michigan won 20–14.

"I can assure you that you will be proud of our young people in the classroom, in the community and most especially in 310 days in Ann Arbor, Michigan, on the football field." —smug former coach Jim Tressel, speaking at an Ohio State basketball game after he had just been hired in 2001 as the football coach at OSU

"They put their pants on one leg at a time, same as everybody else." —Ohio State coach Francis Schmidt, before the 1934 game, with the inception of arguably the dumbest cliché of all time

"Muck Fichigan." —seen on T-shirts all over the OSU campus. You stay classy, Columbus.

"I wanted that undefeated season more than anything I ever wanted in my life. I'd give anything—my house, my bank account, anything but my wife and family—to get it." —on his quest for a sixth "official" national championship

"Son, women give birth to babies every day of the year, but we will only once play this game against SMU." —in 1968 to defensive end Mike Radtke, whose wife had just had twins

"I used to say that three things can happen on a forward pass, two of them bad. I don't say that anymore, because I found out four things can happen on a forward pass. The fourth thing is, you can get fired."

"I never knew of a newspaper man winning a game for us yet."

"But when you see officials decide a ballgame, I'm bitter. So I went out there to let them know I was bitter. That's why I don't like officials."

"I've got more important things to do than sit around and answer charges that are ridiculous." —when questioned about recruiting allegations in 1976

"It's only right that I do so. It's not that I'm paying these kids to play football. I'm just helping out occasionally in private and individual cases on their merits. I see nothing wrong with it." —on the 1956 allegations

"Fumbles have to be psychological."

"You are going down to the Lombardi Award thing in Houston, but don't get too excited. They won't give it to no Yankee bastard." —to Jim Stillwagon

"If those SOBs want to fight the Civil War all over again, we'll certainly do it." —pregame speech, 1978 Gator Bowl vs. Clemson

Woody on Life/Society

"Football is about the only unifying force left in America today. It is certainly one of the few places in our society where teamwork, mental discipline, and the value of hard work still mean anything. We stick to the old-fashioned virtues, and if the rest of the country had stuck to them, it would have been a different story in Vietnam."

"I see my job as a part of American civilization and a damn important part. I see football as being just so much above everything else."

"We're tearing down all of our heroes in America."

"This game of football used to be pretty important to me. It isn't anymore. Now it's damn near everything. It represents and embodies everything that's great about this country, because the United States is built on winners, not losers or people who don't bother to play."

"They've gotten so goddamned liberal up there at Oberlin they don't even give a shit about sports anymore. I hear they're even letting women in their sports program now. That's your Women's Liberation, boy—bunch of goddamned lesbians."

"Loyalty is a two-way street, not a blind alley."

"Sure marijuana will help 'em graduate. Graduate to cocaine!"

"The Russians can't beat us at anything—they can't even feed themselves."

Woody on Himself

"Feeling cold is psychological."

"Nobody despises to lose more than I do. That's what got me into trouble over the years, but it also made a man with mediocre ability a pretty good coach."

"All my life I've always been and always will be a hero-worshiper."

"You have no more right to tell me how to coach my team in front of 15 other writers than I would have to tell you how to write your stories in front of 15 other coaches." —to writers during Michigan week, 1954

"I don't like nice people. I like tough, honest people."

"I'm not the Cadillac type." —turning down a free car

"I had a Cadillac offered to me a couple of times. You know how that works. They give you a Cadillac one year, and the next year they give you the gas to get out of town."

"Get the hell away from me! I can do it myself." —to Jim Parker, who tried to help him cross the street

"Should I apologize for all the good things that I've done?" —on apologizing for the Bauman incident

"Meet me at the racquetball court in half an hour. If you're not there, it's because you can't take it." —to Bo Schembechler

"I did it for my players. I owed it to them and I would have been derelict in my duty to them if I had done less." —on the 1971 Michigan incident

"I can't be nice and win. It's not my way."

"Now I want to tell you that people need friends. I visited an old friend today, Dick Nixon. Right now, he has no friends. Nobody wants to be friends with him, but I am still Dick's friend. Dick can count on Woody. Woody will be there for Dick Nixon."

"You don't have to like me, just respect me."

"You know something. Those 56 percent probably weren't even living when I started here. No, I'm not interested. It's more what I'm going to do, and I'm not going to worry much over that. Sure, people are fickle, and I don't much care. There's no one in this league or in any other league that has won as many games as I have. I'm not going to let their opinion decide this thing. And if you're one of the 56 percent, I don't give a damn about you either." —when told in 1978 that a poll found that 56 percent of Columbus residents thought he should retire

Woody on Michigan

"I read your book, you SOB!" —holding up Bo Schembechler's book after the 1970 game

"How did our great rivalry get started? Well, the real fight started back in 1836 when Andrew Jackson, that wily old cuss, took Toldeo away from that state up north and gave it to us."

"I didn't like that SOB when he played for me, I didn't like him when he worked for me, and I certainly don't like him now." —on Bo Schembechler

"They're traitors! They're traitors!" —talking about sportswriters from the OSU student paper the *Lantern* after they picked OSU to lose to Michigan in 1971

"We don't give a damn for the whole state of Michigan."

MEAN STREAK

Hayes was an enigma, that's for sure. But, again, his temper was his undoing. And the incident in the Gator Bowl wasn't a first-time thing, it was the straw that broke the camel's back. Hayes' volatile legacy dates back to at least 1956 when, following a loss to USC, Hayes allegedly threw a punch at one sportswriter but hit another person by mistake. In 1965 Hayes nearly started a fight with Iowa athletics director Forest Evashevski at the Big Ten ADs and Coaches meeting. In 1971 against Michigan, Hayes—livid over what he perceived was a non-call for pass interference by a Michigan player—ran onto the field and confronted referee Jerry Markbreit, ripped up sideline markers, threw a penalty flag back onto the field, and had to be restrained by fellow coaches and team officials. He was ejected from that game and later suspended for a game and fined $1,000 by the Big Ten. In 1973, at the Rose Bowl, Hayes shoved a camera into the face of a photographer, was suspended for three games the following season, and fined $2,000. And, finally, in 1978, came the incident with Charlie Bauman.

Ohio State was trailing the 1978 Gator Bowl to Clemson 17–15 with about two and a half minutes to play, but was driving behind freshman quarterback Art Schlichter. The Buckeyes were deep into Clemson territory when, in a shocking bit of irony, Hayes—Mr. Three Yards and a Cloud of Dust—called for a pass. Schlichter dropped back and was under a bit of pressure and threw a short pass off his back foot. He never saw Bauman, a nose guard who faked a rush and then dropped back into coverage.

Bauman intercepted the pass and raced up the left sideline, the Ohio State sideline. It was Schlichter who chased down Bauman and made the tackle with two teammates, all of whom slid a couple of feet into the OSU sideline. Now, OSU fans over the years have tried to justify Hayes' actions by saying that Bauman taunted the Buckeyes. But unless it happened in a nanosecond, and it was verbal, nothing happened. Bauman did pop up immediately after the tackle and stare at the OSU players. But in the same moment—literally, the same heartbeat—the video shows Hayes' left hand reaching for the back of Bauman's jersey and his right hand coming around to punch Bauman in the throat, triggering a brawl.

OSU offensive lineman Ken Fritz tried to restrain Hayes in the aftermath, but Hayes fought back against his own player and had to be restrained by defensive coordinator George Hill.

The game was televised by ABC, and, as the play developed, announcer Keith Jackson called the interception correctly but said he didn't know what triggered the brawl. When ABC went to the video replay, for some reason it froze right as Hayes was about to punch Bauman, prompting announcer Keith Jackson to say, "Well, you can't tell there. I don't see anything that would have triggered it except a lot of glum faces."

There was a 15-yard unsportsmanlike conduct called, but the announcers did not say who it was against. Clemson then ran one play, a running play, and as the camera panned to the time counting down to 1:43, a great roar could be heard, and Jackson then said, "Uh-oh! Now we got an official and Woody Hayes involved here!" Buckeyes All-America line-backer Tom Cousineau came running over to his own side-line and threw his hands up as if to say, *What the hell?* and he appeared to be looking right at Hayes. Again, Hill had to play peacemaker, first pushing Cousineau back out on the playing field and then standing between Hayes and the ref-erees as another 15-yard unsportsmanlike conduct penalty was assessed.

As the clock ticked down to zero, Hayes took off his trademark block "O" baseball cap and his glasses, and walked across the field. It would be the last game of his career. According to the January 8, 1979, edition of *Sports Illustrated*:

> Ohio State Athletic Director Hugh Hindman, who had
> played for Hayes at Miami University in 1949 and served

TOP 10 MOST UNSPORTSMANLIKE MOMENTS IN SPORTS
(according to ESPN)

10. Chicago Bull Dennis Rodman kicks a photographer in the groin after falling out of bounds in a game against Minnesota.
9. In a 1997 IRL race at Texas Motor Speedway, car owner A.J. Foyt attacks driver Arie Luyendyk, who had crashed the winner's circle of Foyt's driver.
8. In 1997 Michael Westbrook attacked his own player, pounding running back Stephen Davis.
7. Also in 1997, Denver Broncos linebacker Bill Romanowski spits in the face of San Francisco wideout J.J. Stokes.
6. Lakers forward Kermit Washington sucker punches Rockets forward Rudy Tomjanovich in a 1977 game.
5. In 1993 Dale Hunter rammed Pierre Turgeon into the boards after Turgeon scored, earning a 21-game suspension.
4. Pawtucket Red Sox outfielder Izzy Alcantara went to charge the mound against Wilkes-Barre pitcher Blas Cedeno—but not before turning around and kicking catcher Jeremy Salazar with a karate-style kick.
3. Back to the NHL, Marty McSorley earns a 23-game suspension for whacking Donald Brashear.
2. Mike Tyson nearly bites Evander Holyfield's ear clear off in a title fight.
1. The Woody Hayes incident, with the ESPN announcer saying, "Sadly, nobody remembers Woody Hayes' three national titles and four Rose Bowl wins because of this incident in the '78 Gator Bowl."

OHIO STATE

as one of his assistants at Ohio State for seven years, confronted Hayes privately in the locker room. Hindman told Hayes he was going to inform the Ohio State president, who was in the stands, of the particulars of the affray, and that Hayes "could expect the worst possible result." There was a bitter exchange between the two men, and then, Hindman says, Hayes "asked if he had the opportunity to resign, and I told him he did. Shortly thereafter he said, 'I'm not going to resign. That would make it too easy for you. You had better go ahead and fire me.'" With that, Hindman drove off to see Ohio State President Harold L. Enarson at the country club in Ponte Vedra where he was staying. They met shortly after two in the morning, and Hindman told Enarson, who had no clear idea of what had happened on the field, about Hayes. They agreed to fire him. "There isn't a university or an athletic conference in the country which would permit a coach to physically assault a college athlete," Enarson says. At 8:00 AM Hindman told Hayes he was through as coach. After returning to Columbus, Hayes cleared out his office of his few personal possessions, including his books on Emerson, great generals and wars, loaded them into his Bronco, and went home to seclusion.

Sports Illustrated noted in the same article that, "It is surprising that Hayes was not canned years ago. In addition to numerous publicized outbursts of temper and violence, Hayes often flew into ungovernable rages in practice and struck his players. There was talk last year that Ohio State wanted to fire Hayes after he punched an ABC cameraman in the stomach, but it was just talk; the only punishment meted out to Hayes was a year's 'probation' by the Big Ten."

New York Times columnist Red Smith wrote, "Evidently nobody in authority realized that a full-grown man who attached such importance to a game was, at best, immature, not to say a case of arrested development. The saddest part of the whole affair is that nobody at Ohio State saw the denouement approaching and protected Hayes from himself."

As for Bauman, he has unfairly lived with the moniker that he was the man who got Woody Hayes fired. In 2009, in a story in the *Jacksonville Times-Union* on the 30th anniversary of the punch, Bauman—who now lives in Ohio, of all places—said, "Why can't people let it rest?"

He was asked about the ABC telecast, in which announcer Jackson and color analyst Ara Parseghian, the former Notre Dame coaching legend, did not address the incident, claiming they didn't see it. Bauman said, "I believe they saw it. They covered it up."

Bauman said he just wishes the incident would go away. "If nothing else happened after the interception, nobody would have ever remembered it," he said. "It's really no big deal. It wasn't a big deal for me then; it's not a big deal now.... I don't have anything bad to say about Coach Hayes. He made a mistake. We all make mistakes. I mean, he didn't hurt me or anything."

Only his own reputation.

JIM TRESSEL

We were trying to figure out if we hated Jim Tressel for the 9–1 record in 10 years against Michigan, or for the corrupt program he ran. Then we realized he's 9–1 against Michigan *because* his program was corrupt.

Jim Tressel watches a spring football game on April 23, 2011, one of his last games as head coach. He resigned in May 2011 because he lied and cheated.

Wait, we'll stop here, Ohio State fans, as you try to defend Tattoo Gate—and Tressel's deception and flat-out lies—not to mention Maurice Clarett and Troy Smith.

Waiting.... Waiting, sweetheart, waiting.

Okay, sorry, we don't have that kind of time to listen to nonsense.

Ohio State fans were all over Michigan when it was revealed the Wolverines, under then-coach Rich Rodriguez, conducted unauthorized practices and weight training sessions prior to the 2010 season. Well, Pot, meet Kettle. Kettle, Pot.

Jim Tressel grew up in Mentor, Ohio, a quarterback who ended up playing college ball for his father at Baldwin-Wallace in Berea, Ohio. He was pretty good, too, earning four varsity letters while being named all-conference as a senior. He then became a football coach, working as an assistant at Akron, Miami of Ohio, and Syracuse before becoming the quarterbacks and receivers coach at Ohio State in 1983.

After three seasons as a Buckeyes assistant, he was named the head coach at Youngstown State. There, Tressel compiled a record of 135–57–2 from 1986 through 2000, winning four NCAA Division I-AA national championships. And, lest Buckeyes fans think—as they always do—that Tressel's issues at OSU were a one-time anomaly, it was at Youngstown State where Tressel first ran into trouble with the NCAA. According to an espn.com investigation:

> Star quarterback Ray Isaac was taking money from a booster from virtually the moment he joined the team in 1988. A few hundred here, a thousand or so there, including $3,800 during the 1991 championship season. In all, Isaac got about $10,000, plus the use of various cars, during his career. Ray "the Colonel" Isaac was Tressel's original Maurice Clarett, a Youngstown kid with quick

feet and open palms who would lift his team, and coach, to new heights. Isaac's benefactor was Michael "Mickey" Monus, chairman of the university's board of trustees and the CEO of the rapidly expanding Phar-Mor discount drug store chain.… This much is certain, based on an ESPN review of legal documents and other sources: Monus was no stranger to Tressel. A huge sports fan, Monus could be found on the sidelines during Penguin games. He was on the university athletics committee that hired Tressel. And, according to court testimony that eventually brought the Isaac payments to light, it was Tressel who directed Isaac to Monus at the start of his freshman year.

So Ohio State probably should have operated under the premise of where there's smoke there's fire, but still hired Tressel anyway in 2001 when it fired John Cooper. Now, of course, where there's smoke, there's a raging inferno. In the wake of Tressel's May 2011 resignation, it'll take a massive crew to clean up the debris.

5

WE HATE THEIR CAMPUS, CITY, AND STATE

WELCOME TO COLUMBUS...armpit of the United States.

Really, it's a godawful place. Not nice to visit, and I wouldn't want to live there, either.

And neither did Sandy, a transplant from Huntington, West Virginia, who wrote the following in 2008 on the website best-places.net:

> We moved to Columbus, Ohio, trying to better ourselves and stay somewhat close to family in West Virginia. Before anyone says anything, I did my research. A lot of these sites don't tell you everything, and at times the data isn't completely accurate. On paper, Columbus looked great, but it's not.... Columbus is an aging city that has not kept up with growth. The people generally aren't friendly.... Your neighbors could care less about you. Crime is getting so out of hand. People will shoot you for anything right now, and it's disturbing. Taxes are excessive.... [And] the commute [is] excessive. You can live right on the edge of town, but you're still going to be driving anywhere from 45 minutes

to an hour one way to work. If there is bad weather, you can double that.

No need to go on. Sandy was actually being kind. Columbus is a hole, to be blunt. When you think of Columbus, you think of Ohio State. And when you think of Ohio State, the only thing that comes to mind is the immortal words of the fictional but great Dean Wormer: "Fat, drunk, and stupid is no way to go through life, son."

Columbus is actually the largest city in the state, as well as the state capital. The city is named in honor of Christopher Columbus and was founded in 1812, which is sort of strange since I've been there and can't find a decent Italian joint in the whole damn city. Unless, you know, you're a Columbus resident and consider The Olive Garden to be the definitive Italian restaurant.

Actually, the city does have a replica of one of Christopher Columbus' ships, the *Santa Maria*, sitting on the banks of the scurvy Scioto River. On the website in-and-around-columbus. com, which purportedly gives you a list of things to do in Columbus (all three of them), the site notes, "Operating as it would have over 500 years ago, you get to experience some of what the explorer's [sic] did. Imagine navigating with the equipment they used instead of the high tech equipment we have today." Yeah. Just imagine.

The *Santa Maria* is not even at the top of the list of things "to do" in Columbus, according to in-and-around-columbus. com. Listed at the top, the very top, numero uno, the apparent best thing to do in Columbus is to tour the American

Whistle Corporation. For just $4 per person, the company will take you on a 45-minute tour inside the fascinating world of whistle-making.

Honey?!? Cancel the trip to Disney. We're going to Columbus, baby!

Columbus does have one advantage over Ann Arbor. The city has a professional sports team—it's called the Ohio State football program. (No, I'm not saying that the Buckeyes are paid. That would be against NCAA rules. I'm not saying that at all. I'm implying it, but I'm not saying it.)

Actually, Columbus does have a National Hockey League franchise in the Blue Jackets and a Major League Soccer team in the Crew, which, of course, only add to the boredom on a typical night in Columbus.

There are several Fortune 500 companies located in Columbus, including The Limited. The Limited owns Victoria's Secret, the famed lingerie store. The authors of that other book down south opined that some companies require their employees to live in the city where they work, and wouldn't it be cool if The Limited required its Victoria's Secret supermodels to live in Columbus? Riiiiiight. I can guarantee you that the women who model for Victoria's Secret would sooner sit down and eat a Burger King Triple Whopper (with cheese), fries, and a regular soda, and top it off with a chocolate shake before they would live in Columbus.

To sit here and compare living in Ann Arbor with living in Columbus is a waste of time and, frankly, a waste of space that we could be devoting to more important issues. But, just to make it clear, here are a few tidbits from homefair.com when comparing A2 to Columbus.

	ANN ARBOR	COLUMBUS
Median household income	$79,836	$48,185
Average household income	$81,033	$56,449
Median disposable income	$63,943	$41,245
Sales tax rate	6%	6.75%
Total crime risk	85	128*
Personal crime risk	84	90*
Property crime risk	97	134*

*To explain the crime risk numbers, homefair.com bases these on a comparison to the national average. Using the figure of 100 as the base national average, Columbus' total crime risk is 22 percent greater than the national average—and Ann Arbor's is less, of course.

Besides OSU, other colleges in Columbus are Columbus State Community College, Columbus College of Art and Design, Fortis College, DeVry University, Ohio Business College, Ohio Institute of Health Careers, Bradford School, Franklin University, Bexley Hall Episcopal Seminary, Mount Carmel College of Nursing, Ohio Dominican University, Pontifical College, Josephinum, and Trinity Lutheran Seminary. These schools represent the collective group of colleges that current Ohio State students were not accepted to.

Ohio State was founded in 1870 as a land-grant university, which puts it 53 years behind the founding of the University of Michigan. Its enrollment of 55,014 students on the

RESTAURANTS *AND* BARS WE HATE

BUCKEYE HALL OF FAME GRILL, Columbus, Ohio (officially and pretentiously licensed by OSU, which clearly needs to manufacture a fan base)

THE VARSITY CLUB, Columbus, Ohio

AVERAGE JOE'S, Columbus, Ohio (what, couldn't think of an original name?)

RHINO BAR AND PUMPHOUSE, Washington, D.C. (and a Penn State bar, too)

BLONDIE'S, New York, New York (worse than Rhino— it's a Michigan State bar, too)

OHIO STATE

Columbus campus ensures—and actually enhances—the theory that there's an ass in every bunch. Thousands, in this instance.

Perhaps most galling about the school and what we hate the most is the audacity to call itself "The" Ohio State University. What, like there's another one and you have to distinguish it? Allegedly, that's the answer—to distinguish itself from Ohio University. Of course, we all know this is rooted in a misguided and misplaced overinflated sense of self. It's hysterical to watch NFL games on Sunday and Monday when the players introduce themselves. "John Doe, THE Ohio State University." Really? REALLY? "The" Ohio State University? You mean the one you likely didn't graduate from?

Ohio U, Toledo, Akron, Youngstown State…really, "The" Ohio State University should be reclassified as "An" Ohio State University.

FAMOUS ALUMNI?

Ohio State also likes to boast about its alumni, which includes:

- Two Nobel Laureates, Paul Flory and William A. Fowler (never heard of 'em)
- Poet Mary Oliver (never heard of her)
- FDIC chairman William Isaac (so that's where the country's money problems come from)

PLACES WE HATE

OHIO STADIUM. Perfectly named the Horseshoe for a reason—it smells like a barn.

COLUMBUS, OHIO. See above.

MIRROR LAKE. Apparently, there's some sort of tradition (that's like a whole decade old) of jumping in this lake during Michigan Week. OSU's Office of Student Life warns students on its website that "Mirror Lake is old and dirty," and that "cuts are likely to become infected from all the bacteria in the water." They still jump in. Tools.

THE OVAL. This is sort of OSU's version of the Diag. The only difference is, it's located in front of Ohio State's main library—a place that Buckeyes athletes rarely, if ever, enter.

THE OLENTANGY RIVER. It runs right through the OSU campus. Its original name was *keenhongsheconsepung*, which, as you all know, is Native American for "Our football team is made up mostly of criminals."

OHIO STATE

- Former N.Y. Yankees owner George Steinbrenner (enough said)
- The Limited CEO Leslie Wexner (Victoria's Secret? No argument here)
- Comedian Richard Lewis (his own school once called him "a drunk" in one of OSU's media guides)
- Automobile engineer Charles Kettering (he's no Henry Ford)
- Olympian Jesse Owens (no quibble here; we'll give you that one)
- Golfer Jack Nicklaus (see above)
- Basketball coach Bobby Knight (see above)
- Daniel Amstutz, former head of the International Wheat Council (hey, there's something to be proud of!)
- Carole Black, former president and CEO of Lifetime Entertainment (hot as hell, even today at 67, which begs the question of how she ended up at OSU)
- Grant Devine, former premier of Saskatchewan (which is just as important as being lt. gov. of Utah)
- Patricia Heaton, actress (meh)
- Kirk Herbstreit, ESPN (need we say anything else?)
- Michael R. White, former mayor of Cleveland (speaks for itself)

ONLY IN OHIO

The state of Ohio also has some of the most inane laws in the country, most of which, to our knowledge, are still on the books.

In Ohio, if you ignore an orator on Decoration Day to such an extent as to publicly play croquet or pitch horseshoes within one mile of the speaker's stand, you can be fined $25.

Women are prohibited from wearing patent leather shoes in public. (Can't imagine this is still on the books, but it doesn't prohibit women from wearing their too-short patent leather skirts in public.)

It is illegal to fish for whales on Sunday. (Try Tuesday. Heard that was a good day.)

It is illegal to get a fish drunk. (Which is a shame, of course, considering getting drunk is what they do best there.)

The Ohio driver's education manual states that you must honk the horn whenever you pass another car. (Does that also include giving the one-finger salute?)

Participating in or conducting a duel is prohibited.

Breast-feeding is not allowed in public.

It is illegal for more than five women to live in a house.

It is illegal to mistreat anything of great importance.

No one may be arrested on Sunday or on the Fourth of July. (Those must have been the days when Terrelle Pryor and the boys sold all their memorabilia.)

In Akron, it is illegal to display colored chickens for sale.

In Bay Village, it is illegal to walk a cow down Lake Road. (Every other road is apparently fine.)

In Bexley, ordinance number 223, of 09/09/19 prohibits the installation and usage of slot machines in outhouses. (Lord knows you'd never get some people out of there.)

In Canton, if you lose your pet tiger, you must notify the authorities within one hour. (Seems reasonable.)

Also in Canton, Power Wheels cars may not be driven down the street. (Discriminatory against the four- to eight-year-old population.)

In Lima, any map that does not have Lima clearly stated on the map cannot be sold. (Damn straight!)

In Paulding, a policeman may bite a dog to quiet him. (And thousands of Ohioans are reading this right now saying, "And what's wrong with that?")

6
WE HATE THEIR FANS

FUCK MICHIGAN.

Really? That's the best you can do, Ohio State? You put your little heads together and that's what you came up with to throw on a T-shirt? Wow. Oh, wait. I forgot. Somebody once got really creative and transposed the "F" and the "M" and made up some shirts that say "Muck Fichigan." Wow, again. "Impressive, really," he said, with sarcasm literally dripping from his mouth.

Then again, should we expect any more from an OSU student or fan than the most simple-minded of vulgarities? And should we expect any more from the idiotic judge who, in 1970, ruled that the T-shirt that read "Fuck Michigan" was not obscene and "accurately expressed" the local sentiment regarding the University of Michigan?

But, that's an OSU fan for you.

A Michigan blogger noted that the State Department—yes, that one—often puts out warnings to American travelers to avoid certain places. Could be obvious, like Afghanistan or Iraq, or could be subtle, like certain areas of Mexico because of the drug wars. The bottom line is, these warnings are to be taken seriously, and the places put on these lists should be avoided like the plague.

Like, say, Columbus, Ohio, for instance.

This is all you need to know about the rudest, most vile, completely vulgar, sometimes violent college football fan base in America—in 2006, the University of Michigan had to issue a State Department–like warning to its fans traveling to Ohio State for The Game.

That's not a joke.

> We know that it can be uncomfortable being in an opposing team's environment, especially when the stakes are so high. We would like to offer a few suggestions in order to help you stay safe and have a positive experience this weekend:
> —Try carpooling to the game; if possible, drive a car with non-Michigan license plates.
> —Keep your Michigan gear to a minimum, or wait until you are inside the stadium to display it.
> —Stay with a group.
> —Know and obey the laws regarding alcohol use.
> —If you are of legal age to drink, use alcohol in moderation. Stay in the blue.
> —Stay low-key; don't draw unnecessary attention to yourself.
> —If verbally harassed by opposing fans, don't take the bait.
> —Avoid High Street in Columbus.

If at any time you feel unsafe, you should call 9-1-1 for assistance. U-M campus police also will be available in Columbus to support our fans. You may call them with non-emergency concerns.

We look forward to a tremendous game on Saturday. Let's help the Wolverines win with spirit and class.

Go Blue!

Sue Eklund, Associate Vice President and Dean of Students

Steve Grafton, President, Alumni Association

Nicole Stallings, MSA President

Really? Really. That's how bad it is. The part about the cars and the non-Michigan license plates? It actually borders on comical how often Ohio police—townies and state police—pull over those driving with Michigan plates for such major infractions as doing 43 mph in a 40 mph zone. The part about walking down High Street? It's like being in a third-world country whose citizens burn American flags as a hobby and you're wearing your red, white, and blue jacket.

What's not comical, however, are the OSU fans.

The authors of the Michigan fan site The M Zone (www.michiganzone.blogspot.com) summed it up perfectly with this 2006 analysis:

OHIO STATE—THE RUDEST FANS IN AMERICA

Used to be, I always wanted Ohio State to win every game each season...except one. In fact, leading up to our annual showdown with the Bucks, I never understood Michigan fans cheering with glee whenever I was sitting in the stands at the Big House and the stadium announcer came over the PA system to reveal Ohio State was losing or had been upset. Made no sense to me. Because I didn't want to beat a three- or four-loss OSU squad at the end of the season, I wanted to dash the hopes of an undefeated team playing for something truly meaningful.

And let me also say, like a guy defending himself against charges of being a racist, "Some of my best friends are Buckeyes." One was my roommate for a couple years out of college, one was in my wedding party, and another is a work colleague. All very good friends to this day.

Yet, having said all that, I now hope Ohio State loses every game. Even though it looks bad for the Big Ten, I openly root against them in their bowl games. And it's all for one reason: their fans.

Over the years, I've grown to really dislike Buckeyes fans. And it all stems from one too many bouts of abuse attending games in Columbus.

Sweeping generalization? Sure. But once you get attacked and barked at by the neighborhood dog enough, you begin to loathe the creature each time you pass. Hey, there's a reason the Ohio State mascot is a nut: because their fans are crazy. And not in a good way. More in that, "Shit, we had to bail Stank out of jail again after he got into another bar fight last night" way.

Funny thing is, I used to respect Ohio State fans. They love their team and they are *loud*. But, in my five trips to the 'Shoe, they are also the most abusive fans I've ever come in contact with at a sporting event. The things that I've *personally* experienced in Columbus which have brought me to my current feelings are as follows:

• My uncle was once hit in the back by a thrown *full* beer bottle before The Game. Now, maybe whoever threw it was aiming for a trash can somewhere, but I think it might have had something to do with the maize and blue color of his jacket.

• A few years before it burned down in '96, I was at Papa Joe's, an Ohio State watering hole, the night before the big game when a waitress ran over to me and advised me to turn my Michigan shirt inside out. I thought she was joking. She wasn't. Said it wasn't safe. When I actually asked if she was joking, she shook her head and said it would be the "same if a Buckeyes fan was wearing an Ohio State shirt in Ann Arbor." Not that she believed me (or any Ohio State fans reading this will), but I told her, actually, it was *very* different.

MOVIES *AND* TV SHOWS WE HATE

We have no dislike for any movie or TV show featuring Ohio State. Mostly because we couldn't find any movie or TV show featuring that school down south. Wait, that's a lie. We found one.

BABY BUCKEYE. An "adorable, fun-filled introduction to The Ohio State University Buckeyes." Saw it on Amazon, and it's been discontinued. Obviously. You don't want to scar kids for life, do you?

• Before the 2002 game, when a win would send OSU to the BCS title game in Tempe, it seemed every fan in Columbus was carrying a bag of Tostitos (or making a fashion statement by wearing an empty one on their heads). Well, before kickoff, I was standing on Lane Avenue near the Varsity Club when a group (plural) of rather large Buckeyes fans spotted the Michigan shirt under my jacket (for safety purposes, I had given up wearing a Michigan jacket when my uncle got pelted with the beer bottle). One of them ran up to me and threw a handful of Tostitos in my face. I felt my fist clench but, being surrounded by, oh, about 10,000 Buckeyes, I realized whatever swing I got in would be my last. And, hey, the Buckeyes guy was really cool. He just laughed, went to wipe the Tostitos off, and said, "Hey, man, I'm just fucking with you." Gee, thanks, dick.

• I have been flipped off and told to fuck a) myself, b) Michigan, and c) numerous other things more times than I can possibly count while walking near the 'Shoe on game day. And while I expect it from the drunk frat guy crowd, I'm always surprised when it's a coed or the elderly. (Along those lines, another 2004 incident too "good" not to share is, after we lost, Benny, Wangs, and I were rushing out of the 'Shoe with seconds left in order to beat the crowd. Passing an elderly couple (70+), the *woman*, seeing our M gear, shouted, "Go back to Michigan, you big losers!" Couldn't believe it.) As I tell people all the time, the thing that always surprises me the most is that I hear "Fuck Michigan!" more than "Go Bucks!" before The Game in Columbus.

Again, those are my personal, firsthand experiences in Columbus over the years. And I'm not alone. My friend who was in the Michigan Marching Band told me about dodging debris and loogies as they took the field. We all know about the Michigan team bus being subjected to drug/bomb sniffing dogs in '04. And, lest one think it's strictly M fans that get such special treatment in Columbus due to our long-festering rivalry, Texas fans were treated so poorly that the OSU president wrote an apology to one Texas fan.

The ironic thing is, get Buckeyes away from the 'Shoe, and they seem like nice folks. But put them within a few square miles of the stadium on a football Saturday, and mob rule takes over. I'm sure theories abound, but I honestly wonder why that is. And as stories continue to mount (like the Texas mention above), the university sincerely needs to address this problem before somebody gets seriously hurt. Whether they want to admit it or not, there is a problem in Columbus on game days.

Funniest Columbus Memory: In town for what turned out to be John Cooper's final M–OSU game, one of the local radio stations was only playing songs from years in which Ohio State beat Michigan. But, since Coop had only won The Game twice in 13 years, it was like listening to an oldies station. I don't know who came up with that idea and thought it was a good one, but as a Michigan fan, it was hilarious. And I've never heard so many Beatles tunes on a top 40 station before in my life!

Of course, one of the things we *love* about OSU fans is how easy it is to make fun of them. File these away for the next time you encounter those lovely folks from Columbus:

Q: How many Ohio State students does it take to change a light bulb?
A: One, but he gets three credits.

Q: What does the average Ohio State football player get on his SAT?
A: Drool.

Four college alumni were climbing a mountain. There was an Ohio State grad, a Michigan grad, a Penn State grad, and a Notre Dame grad. Each proclaimed to be the most loyal of all fans at their alma mater. As they climbed higher, they argued as to which of them was the most loyal of all. They continued to argue all the way up the mountain. When they finally reached the top, the Notre Dame grad hurled himself off the mountain, shouting, "This is for the Fighting Irish!" as he fell to his doom. Not wanting to be outdone, the Penn State grad threw himself off the mountain, proclaiming, "This is for the Nittany Lions!" Seeing this, the Michigan grad walked over and shouted, "This is for the Wolverines!" and pushed the Ohio State grad over the side.

Q: You're stranded on a deserted island with three people: a cannibal, a mass murderer, and a guy in an Ohio State hat. You have a gun with only two bullets remaining. Who do you shoot?
A: The Ohio State fan. Twice.

A Michigan fan, an OSU fan, and a pig are all in the waiting room of the hospital waiting for their wives to give birth. All of a sudden the lights go out. When they come back on, the doctor comes out to the three and says, "They are all healthy, but we can't determine which child belongs to which parents. They decide to draw straws and see who is the first dad to go in and try to decide which kid is his. So they draw straws, and the Michigan fan gets the shortest straw, so he goes in first. After about 15 minutes of looking at the three kids, the U-M fan drops his head in disgust and grabs the pig. The doctor asks, "Are you sure you made the correct choice?" The U-M fan replies, "No, but I can't take a chance in getting that damn Ohio State kid."

Q: What's the difference between an Ohio State fan and a carp?
A: One is a bottom-feeding scum-sucker and the other is a fish.

Q: What do you call a hot girl walking around the Ohio State campus?
A: A visitor.

Q: What should you do if you find three Ohio State fans buried up to their neck in cement?
A: Get more cement.

Q: What do you get when you put 32 Ohio State cheerleaders in one room?
A: A full set of teeth

Q: What's the only sign of intelligent life in Columbus?
A: Ann Arbor: 187 Miles

Q: What is the difference between a dead dog on the freeway and a dead Ohio State fan on the freeway?
A: There are skid marks in front of the dog.

Q: How do you get to Columbus from Ann Arbor?

A: Go south until you smell manure, then east until you step in it.

SOURCES

I Love Michigan: Introduction

http://buckeyefansonly.com/thegame.html
http://buckeyefansonly.com/thegamehistoricalperspective.
   html

Quotes

http://espn.go.com/espn/page2/index?id=5854774
http://therealests.blogspot.com/2006/11/grimiest-ohio-state-
   michigan-quotes.html

Games We Love

First Game Ever: http://bentley.umich.edu/athdept/football/
   umosu/1897game.htm
First OSU Win: http://library.osu.edu/projects/
   OSUvsMichigan/news/1919.htm
http://buckeyefansonly.com/thegamehistoricalperspective.html
http://bentley.umich.edu/athdept/football/coaches/fhyost.htm
http://www.annarbor.com/news/1940-tom-harmon-becomes-
   first-michigan-man-to-win-heisman-trophy-crisler-takes-
   blame-for-onl/
http://www.snagfilms.com/films/title/
   rivalries_the_history_of_michigan_vs_ohio_state/
http://www.youtube.com/watch?v=Vskt2_Kd9cQ
http://www.youtube.com/watch?v=kSwmazJBbIU

Players We Love

http://www.usatoday.com/sports/college/football/2007-11-13-
3885402658_x.htm

http://en.wikipedia.org/wiki/Bob_Chappuis

http://en.wikipedia.org/wiki/Whitey_Wistert

http://www.annarbor.com/sports/um-football/catching-up-
with-former-michigan-running-back-tim-biakabutuka/

Traditions We Love

http://thosewhostaywillbechampions.blogspot.com/2007/02/
brief-history-of-go-blue-banner.html

http://www.mgoblue.com/sports/m-footbl/
spec-rel/021910aad.html

The Ten Year War: Ten Classic Games Between Bo and
Woody Copyright 2005, Joel Pennington

http://www.mgoblue.com/sports/m-footbl/
spec-rel/112009aaa.html

Coaches We Love

http://rivalryfootball.com/quotes/bo-schembechler-quotes/

http://www.goodreads.com/author/quotes/14642.
Bo_Schembechler

http://www.nytimes.com/1995/05/05/sports/college-football-
moeller-resigns-as-michigan-coach.html

We Love Our Stadium

http://bentley.umich.edu/athdept/stadium/stadtext/ufer.htm

We Love Our Campus and City

http://www.hr.umich.edu/um/um-isms.html

Marching Band Sidebar

http://mmb.music.umich.edu/history/falcone.asp

I Hate Ohio State: Introduction
http://genuinelysarcastic.blogspot.com

Players We Hate
http://www.ohiostatebuckeyes.com/ViewArticle.
    dbml?DB_OEM_ID=17300&ATCLID=1146055

Coaches We Hate
http://www.ohiohistorycentral.org/entry.php?rec=2147
http://sportsillustrated.cnn.com/vault/article/magazine/
    MAG1094478/index.htm
http://jacksonville.com/sports/college/other_college_sports/
    2008-12-29/gator_bowl_30th_anniversary_punch
http://sports.espn.go.com/ncf/news/story?id=6194162

We Hate Their Fans
http://michiganzone.blogspot.com/2006/01/best-and-worst-
    college-football-fans.html

ACKNOWLEDGMENTS

WELL, LET'S START WITH THE OBVIOUS—the good folks at Triumph Books, who not only provided guidance but also showed the patience of Job when yours truly was *way* beyond deadline for turning this in. Special kudos to one of my old newspaper bosses and good friend, Steve Greenberg, who suggested to Triumph that they reach out to me to author this tome. Greenie, you're a good man, even though you're an Ohio State fan.

Shout-outs, in no particular order: to Jade and the crew at the On A Roll Deli in Highland, New York, who always had lunch ready when I took a break from writing; to Sean and Lou, owners of Coach's Food and Spirits in Millbrook, New York, who always had a beer ready when I needed to blow off steam from writing; to Bruce Springsteen, who always had the right music ready late at night when I needed to keep writing; to the University of Michigan, for, among other things, sending three graduates on the Apollo 15 mission while Ohio State students to this day are still deciphering what the traffic light colors mean; and, finally, to Ohio State. From your insane coaches (Hi Woody!) to your inept coaches (Hi Coop!) to your insincere coaches (Hi Tress!), from your incomprehensible rule-breaking players (Hi Terrelle!) to your inbred peopleofwalmart.com fan base (Hi, um, everybody in Columbus!), all I can say is a heartfelt thank you for making the flip side of this book so easy to write.

ABOUT THE AUTHOR

RICH THOMASELLI CELEBRATED HIS 25th year as a sports journalist on June 24, 2011, and is a nine-time writing award winner. He did not graduate from the University of Michigan but adopted the Wolverines at an early age as his favorite college team and then had the great fortune to later spend four years at the *Ann Arbor News*, covering U-M football and basketball. He has been married to the former Patricia Corbett since 1996 and has two sons, Joe and Dan. Rich hopes both boys someday earn scholarships to Michigan because $40K is a lot to pay for out-of-state students. (The family lives in New York. You got a !@&*%$# problem with that?!?)

I
LOVE
MICHIGAN

RICH THOMASELLI

TRIUMPH
BOOKS

Library of Congress Cataloging-in-Publication Data
Thomaselli, Rich, 1964–
  I love Michigan, I hate Ohio State / Rich Thomaselli.
    p. cm.
  ISBN 978-1-60078-577-1
  1. Michigan Wolverines (Football team)—Miscellanea. 2. University of Michigan—Football—Miscellanea. 3. Ohio State Buckeyes (Football team)—Miscellanea. 4. Ohio State University—Football—Miscellanea. I. Title.
  GV958.M52T56 2011
  796.332'630977—dc23
                        2011026607

This book is available in quantity at special discounts for your group or organization. For further information, contact:

Triumph Books
542 South Dearborn Street
Suite 750
Chicago, Illinois 60605
(312) 939-3330
Fax (312) 663-3557
www.triumphbooks.com

Printed in U.S.A.
ISBN: 978-1-60078-577-1
Editorial production by Prologue Publishing Services, LLC
Photos courtesy of AP Images unless otherwise noted

First, to my beautiful family—my wife Trish and my sons, Joseph and Daniel. I am grateful that they allowed me to pursue this project; too often during a six-month span they heard, "Sorry guys, I can't go to (fill-in-the-blank) with you, I'm writing." And they understood. My wife just "gets it" when it comes to being the spouse of a sportswriter, and she has for 15 amazing years now. She is a one-woman support system, a champion of my work, a confidante, and more. She is the dream-maker—she lets me chase them and then helps make them come true. My children are 10 and six at the time of this writing, young enough that they don't quite yet grasp the depth and passion of Michigan–Ohio State, but old enough to yell "Go Blue!" with the best of them. They also have a burning aversion to anything scarlet and gray.

And to head coach Lloyd Carr, his staff, and the 1997 University of Michigan national champions. Carr will certainly find this dedication somewhat surprising, as will some of the players, I'm sure. The head coach and I butted heads several times during my four years as a sportswriter for the Ann Arbor News. But after more than 25 years as a journalist in which I covered Super Bowls, World Series, NCAA Tournaments, professional boxing, golf, and anything and everything you could possibly think of, I look back on that five months from August training camp to the January 1, 1998, Rose Bowl with fond memories. It was the coolest, most fun career ride I've ever been on. Thanks for the lift, fellas.

CONTENTS

INTRODUCTION
WHY WE LOVE MICHIGAN

A guy walks into a bar and sits down to have a couple of beers. After a bit, he strikes up a conversation with a man sitting next to him. They talk weather, they talk politics, they talk sports, and when the conversation rolls around to college football, the guy says to his new friend, "Hey, you wanna hear an Ohio State joke?"

The man stands up, points to two friends sitting on the other side of him, and says, "Well, before you tell any jokes, you should know something. I'm 6', 200 pounds, and I'm an Ohio State graduate. The guy next to me here is 6'2", 225, and he graduated from Ohio State. And the guy next to him is 6'5", 250, and he graduated from Ohio State. Now...you still want to tell that joke?"

The guy who originally walked into the bar looks at the three men, sizes them up, and says, "Well, no, not if I have to explain it three times."

Ah, I got a million of 'em, a million, I tell you.

Such is part and parcel of the rivalry between the University of Michigan and the presumptuously named "The" Ohio State University.

It was first played in 1897—six years before the first World Series was even conceived, 25 years before the National Football League even came into existence. It has become, simply, The Game. It was born from the proximity of neighboring states, grew in stature over several decades as it often decided the Big Ten Conference championship, and then was launched even further into a white-hot, passionate rivalry under two supremely intense coaches.

It is not just the greatest rivalry in college football; it is one of the greatest rivalries in all of sports.

Says who? Says many.

In 1999, when it chronicled the last 100 years of sports as we headed into a new century, ESPN called the Michigan–Ohio State game the greatest rivalry in sports, saying,

> When Ohio Stadium opened in 1922, Michigan spoiled the party with a 22–0 victory. The rivalry was heated in the early days as both have been longtime college football powers. But it got even hotter in 1969, when Bo Schembechler took over as Michigan's coach and upset Woody Hayes' No. 1–ranked, undefeated Buckeyes. Four times in the next six years, both teams were ranked in the top five when they met. In 1970 and 1973 both were undefeated (they tied 10–10 in '73). From 1970 through 1975, Michigan entered without a loss every year. The Wolverines won just once. Ohio State was 9–0–1 in 1993, 11–0 in 1995, and 10–0 in 1996. The Buckeyes lost each time. *That* is rivalry.

Says who else? How about the United State Congress?

In House Resolution 460.IH, adopted on November 20, 2003, to recognize the 100th meeting between Michigan and Ohio State, Congress wrote:

> Whereas on November 22, 2003, the Ohio State Buckeyes will visit the Michigan Wolverines at Michigan Stadium in the 100th meeting between the two football teams: Now, therefore, be it
>> Resolved, That the House of Representatives—
>> (1) congratulates The Ohio State University Buckeyes and the University of Michigan Wolverines on the 100th football game of their rivalry; and
>> (2) recognizes The Ohio State University Buckeyes and the University of Michigan Wolverines football game as the greatest sports rivalry in history.

Q: How do you get an Ohio State graduate off your front porch?
A: Pay him for the pizza.

Q: What did the OSU grad say to the Michigan grad?
A: "Welcome to McDonalds. May I take your order please?"

Earle Bruce, who was an assistant under Woody Hayes from 1972 to 1978 and then head coach from 1979 to 1987, once said, "If you don't win the Michigan–Ohio State game, that's a problem.... You're not going to be recognized for too much success. We've had 11–1 and 10–1 football teams that lost to Michigan, and they're not even mentioned in the second breath."

For better or worse, it's true. Bruce lost his job as OSU's coach, and he even had a winning mark (5–4) against the Wolverines.

His successor, John Cooper, was 2–10–1 against Michigan and was finally ushered out and replaced by Jim Tressel, who, as you may have heard, won't have the chance to continue his 9–1 streak versus U-M. Coincidental or not, Michigan's Bump Elliott was let go after the 1968 season when the Buckeyes beat the snot out of Michigan 50–14 en route to the national championship. And, more recently, Rich Rodriguez was fired as head coach of the Wolverines after the worst three-year period of any at Michigan, including three losses to Ohio State by a combined 76 points.

The Game makes and breaks careers, makes and breaks stars.

"Legends are made in this game," Ohio State offensive guard T.J. Downing said in 2006 before the famous No. 1 versus No. 2 game of unbeaten teams. "Every guy knows they have a chance to go down in the record books and make history."

It was always a competitive rivalry, even though much of it has been somewhat cyclical in nature. Heading into the 2011 season, for instance, Ohio State has won nine of the last 10 games against Michigan. Michigan opened the rivalry by going 13–0–2 in the first 15 games the two schools played during the leather helmet era, and the Wolverines won 10 of 13 during the late 1980s and into the 1990s, when Cooper coached OSU.

The two programs beat the crap out of each other on the field and in recruiting. Both have gone into each other's state to try to convince star players to risk the wrath of their hometowns and play college football in enemy territory. Michigan coaches have been known to rent cars with license plates from

any state other than Michigan. Ohio State? Well, everyone knows that Hayes always referred to Michigan as "that team up north." Legend has it that during a recruiting trip to Michigan, Hayes and an assistant coach were driving back to Ohio in a snowstorm that was progressively getting worse. Hayes was asleep in the passenger seat when the assistant woke him to say they were getting low on fuel and he was just going to stop for gas. Hayes told him to keep driving. A little while later, the assistant again nudged Hayes, who flashed his legendary temper. "No, goddamn it! We do *not* pull in and fill up. And I'll tell you exactly why we don't. It's because I don't buy one goddamn drop of gas in the state of Michigan! We'll coast and *push* this goddamn car to the Ohio line before I give this state a nickel of my money!"

Now *that's* a rivalry.

In fact, it was Hayes who, in part, helped launch the rivalry into the stratospheric consciousness of the country. For many years, Michigan–Ohio State had been a nice Midwest regional rivalry. The nation was consumed still by baseball and, surprise, surprise, boxing. Arnie Palmer still had his Army, and another Ohio State guy, Jack Nicklaus, was drawing tremendous coverage in golf. The NFL was still decades away from even the remote beginnings of the popularity it enjoys today, and college football was dominated nationally by coverage of Notre Dame.

In 1968, against the backdrop of a country reeling internally from the Vietnam War and the Civil Rights movement, Ohio State hosted Michigan in the annual game. The Buckeyes were en route to the national championship that season; the

Wolverines were easy prey and, in fact, they were routed by the Buckeyes 50–14.

But it was that final touchdown that proved to be historical. Leading 44–14, the Buckeyes scored to make it 50–14. Instead of kicking the extra point, Hayes shocked everybody by deciding to go for two in the waning moments of a game already firmly tucked in the "W" category. When asked after the game why he went for the two-point conversion, Hayes said, "Because I couldn't go for three."

It wasn't the first time Hayes had pulled something like this. In the 1961 game in Ann Arbor, he left his starters in late in a 50–20 victory over Michigan. Ironically, though the Buckeyes won the Big Ten championship and a berth in the Rose Bowl, the school's faculty council turned down the bid from the folks in Pasadena, saying that the football program was becoming too big at Ohio State and something had to be done to curb that.

And, to be fair, Michigan had its sportsmanship issues during the rivalry, once kicking a field goal with a 55–0 lead late in the 1946 game at Ohio Stadium.

But it was the ballsy—some would say vindictive—move by Hayes in the '68 game that set in motion a series of events that escalated the rivalry. Bump Elliott was removed as Michigan coach, and a former Hayes assistant at OSU who was the head coach at Miami of Ohio, Glenn E. "Bo" Schembechler, was hired to coach the Wolverines starting with the 1969 season.

And so began the famous Ten-Year War between Bo and Woody, Woody and Bo, that ended only when Hayes was fired

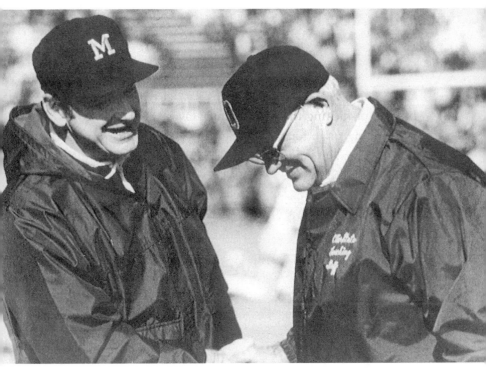

The Ten-Year War began when Bo Schembechler (left) started as head coach at Michigan in 1969. The former assistant to Woody Hayes (right) won the war, with his teams boasting a 11–9–1 record over OSU in The Game.

following the infamous incident in the 1978 Gator Bowl in which he punched a player from Clemson.

The two-point conversion was still very much an issue in Ann Arbor heading into the 1969 game, but the odds still looked daunting. Ohio State brought a 22-game winning streak into the game with a team that Hayes maintained for the rest of his life was the greatest team he ever coached. The Buckeyes were a 17-point favorite, but Michigan pulled off a 24–12 win

so stunning that ABC announcer Bill Flemming called it the "upset of the century."

It was a good day to love Michigan.

It was a great day to hate Ohio State.

> *A young man hired by a supermarket reported for his first day of work. The manager greeted him with a warm handshake and a smile, gave him a broom, and said, "Your first job will be to sweep the store."*
>
> *The young man looked at him incredulously and said, "I played football and graduated from Ohio State."*
>
> *"Oh, I'm sorry. I didn't know that," the manager said. "Here, give me the broom. I guess I'll have to show you how."*

What is it about a rivalry that ignites such passion?

What is it about Michigan–Ohio State that transcends the football field?

Hayes disliked Michigan so much that he not only wouldn't buy gas in the state, he sometimes had his team stay in Toledo—just 45 minutes from Ann Arbor but firmly on the Ohio side of the border—the night before an away game at U-M.

A Columbus, Ohio, judge in 1970 dismissed an obscenity charge against a young man who was arrested for wearing a T-shirt that said "Fuck Michigan." The judge proclaimed that the T-shirt "accurately expressed" feelings within the Columbus community regarding the state and University of Michigan.

Yeah, it's that passionate.

The Michigan–Ohio State game, since 1935, has always been scheduled for the third or fourth Saturday in November. With very few exceptions, it has been the last game of the regular season for both teams, although both schools have, on occasion, enjoyed an extra game on the slate, as Michigan did when it played at Hawaii a week after the OSU game in 1998.

But with at least two-plus months and 10 games separating both teams from their appointed yearly date with destiny, you would think their respective attention spans would be elsewhere.

You would think.

"It was our strategy here at Michigan to do something to beat Ohio State every day," Schembechler said during the 2006 Michigan–Ohio State week, just days before he died on the eve of the big game.

"To me, Michigan is the team you set out at the beginning of the year to beat," two-time Heisman Trophy winner Archie Griffin told Bucknuts.com. "Certainly, you want to win them all, but that is a special game. It is our rival. We want to play a great game against the University of Michigan. It's at the end of the year, and you have all year to improve to be at your best by the time you come to play the Michigan football team."

"Well, you know, I think that rivalry is special," Brady Hoke said on January 12, 2011, the day he was introduced as Michigan's new head coach. "It's like none other in football. Being

STATS WE LOVE

Michigan has won 11 national championships to Ohio State's seven.

The Wolverines have made 20 Rose Bowl appearances to OSU's 14.

U-M's 884 victories are the most in college football history.

Michigan has won 42 Big Ten championships; Ohio State has 35.

57–44–6—Michigan's record versus the Buckeyes in The Game.

engaged in that battle for eight years [as an assistant under Lloyd Carr], and growing up in the state [of Ohio], you knew. Bo and Woody, the great fights they had. It is the most important game on that schedule. And not that the others aren't important, but it is the most important game on that schedule and how we play the game and how we prepare. So it's very important. It's almost personal."

> Q: *Why is ice no longer available at Ohio State football games?*
> A: *Because the senior who knew the recipe finally graduated.*
>
> Q: *What are the three longest years of a Ohio State football player's life?*
> A: *His freshman year.*

So, how does yours truly figure into all of this? Well, I covered the University of Michigan football and basketball programs

from 1996 through 2000 for the *Ann Arbor News*, as well as covering the Big Ten during that same time period for *Sporting News* magazine.

Truth be told, I was already a Michigan fan.

My father had an immense amount of respect for two coaches who he believed struck the right cord of discipline with respect and love for the game—Bobby Knight and Bo Schembechler. The first sporting event I can ever remember attending was an Army basketball game at West Point. It was 1970. I was five, and Knight was the head coach of the Cadets, still a year away from taking the Indiana job.

My father was an old-school Italian-American who was a prison guard—back in the day when they were still known as prison guards and not "corrections officers"—and had a very strong sense of discipline and dedication. My basketball allegiances were to Army and then Indiana, and my football loyalty was to the University of Michigan.

Now, did being a fan and then covering the team turn me into a homer for the Wolverines and compromise my journalistic integrity? Hardly. Go and ask any Old Blue, or a longtime U-M official, or any longtime Ann Arbor resident who remembers me writing for the *Ann Arbor News*. Heck, ask Lloyd Carr.

I first met Michigan football coach Lloyd Carr in the spring of 1997. I joined the paper in December of 1996 but dove head-first into basketball. The paper had a main beat writer for football; I was the columnist. At an informal press conference

at Schembechler Hall with just a few writers, I was introduced to Carr by the sports information director, Bruce Madej.

"Lloyd Carr," he said, extending his hand.

"Rich Thomaselli," I said, shaking it.

"Where are you from?" Carr asked.

"New York," I said.

Carr recoiled in mock—I think—horror, pulled his hand back, and said, "Oh, shit."

We all laughed.

I found Carr to be an engaging man, passionate about the University of Michigan, fiercely loyal to his mentor, Bo Schembechler, as well as to his players. Yet it wouldn't take long for us to clash. When Michigan won its 1997 opener against Colorado in impressive fashion, I wrote a column for the next day that basically said, "Big deal. Michigan has a history of playing down to its opponent, so let's see what happens next week when Baylor comes to town in what should be a blowout game. Then we can start talking about the direction of this team."

The Wolverines blew out the Bears, of course, and went on to an undefeated season and a share of the national championship.

In the following two years, I repeatedly angered Carr over a variety of things. First, by writing that the platoon system he was using for quarterbacks Tom Brady and wunderkind Drew

Henson should be scrapped, and Brady should be the starter and play the entire game. I don't claim to have the same kind of knowledge that Carr—or any other coach—has about football, but I just saw something in Brady that I didn't see in Henson. But Henson was a local kid, who set national records in football and baseball while playing high school ball at nearby Brighton, Michigan, and there had been some pressure on Carr for two years to make sure he got the hometown guy in the fold. Of course, as it played out, Brady became one of Michigan's greatest quarterbacks and had since won three Super Bowls. Henson left Michigan abruptly after his junior season to play professional baseball, but couldn't cut it on the diamond or on the gridiron when he tried to go back to football.

I earned Carr's public wrath on the opening day of the 1999 season, though it turned out to be a case of mistaken identity. Carr had to discipline two players prior to the season opener against Notre Dame. The players were involved in a misdemeanor back in the spring; as a result, their punishment was both physical (running the steps of Michigan Stadium) and mental (they would not be in the starting lineup and, thus, would not be introduced with the starters prior to the game). I had a local morning drive radio show in Ann Arbor on a sports station that specialized in Michigan talk at that time, and Carr had confused me with another host who said the punishment was weak. After Michigan beat Notre Dame 26–22 in the '99 season opener in Ann Arbor, Carr held his usual postgame press conference. When it was apparent there were no more questions, he usually just said, "Okay?" and got up to leave. This time, though, he stared daggers at me, pointed, and said, "I just hope when you have children, they don't have to go through what you put those two kids through." Naturally, I

was confused about what he meant. It took more than a week to sort out, but we did.

Like Bo, Carr was also passionate about the Rose Bowl and the Ohio State rivalry. I truly believe that if Carr and Schembechler could beat Ohio State every year and go to Pasadena—but would have to give up playing for the national championship—they would do it. During the 1997 season, when Michigan needed to beat the Buckeyes to finish unbeaten and go to the Rose Bowl with a chance to win the national title, Carr held his usual Monday press conference. I started to ask him a question and prefaced it by saying that the Michigan–Ohio State game transcends all, the rivalry is so big. So if Auburn and Alabama could play the Iron Bowl in the middle of the season, if Florida could play Tennessee and Georgia in the middle of the season, why couldn't Michigan and OSU play in the middle of the season? Why does it always have to be the last game in November? Both teams have ruined the other's undefeated seasons so many times, perhaps by playing the game earlier in the season then both would have a chance to recover. After all, if you're going to lose once, it might as well be as early as possible.

Carr looked at me like I had three heads. It was the same look I used to get when I would ask why members of the media couldn't attend practice, which was always closed.

When I decided to leave the *Ann Arbor News* in the spring of 2000, I made an appointment to see Carr in his office. I wanted to say good-bye, to thank him and wish him luck. I also wanted him to sign my Michigan media guide. We chatted for a few minutes, and I said to him, "I know you're not

going to believe this, but now that I'm leaving, I figure I can tell you," and I relayed to him how my father had turned me into a Michigan fan. I'm sure he found it impossible to believe, but for a split-second there I could see his demeanor change. He scribbled in my media guide for a minute, and then picked up the phone and called legendary U-M equipment manager Jon Falk and asked him to come up to the office. When Falk arrived, Carr barked, "We're finally getting rid of Thomaselli." And then, softly, he said, "Jon, take him downstairs and let him pick out whatever he wants."

We shook hands, and I exited the office. Falk stopped briefly to speak with Carr's secretary, which gave me a moment to look in the media guide to see what he had written.

"To Rich: You were tough, but you were fair. Lloyd Carr. PS: Now I can open up practice."

I poked me head back in his office and knocked on the open door.

"Hey, Coach?" I said.

"Now what?" Carr said

"Beat Ohio State."

And for the first time, I think I saw a smile crease Lloyd Carr's face.

That's a rivalry.

1

GAMES WE LOVE

YOU KNOW, WHEN YOU'VE WON 57 of these rivalry games (13 more than Ohio State), and 11 national championships (four more than Ohio State), and more than 800 games overall (dozens more than Ohio State), the success all kind of blends together.

Yes, I just said that with a certain amount of smugness.

Nonetheless, here are 10 games that we absolutely love.

1897

OHIO STATE	0	0	0
MICHIGAN	24	10	34

Ah, you know what they say: you never forget your first. Well, okay, no one is still alive from a game that took place 114 years ago, so we'll just have to rely on the news accounts of the day to trumpet what was the very first game in the great rivalry between Michigan and Ohio State.

By this time, U-M had been playing football for almost 20 years, while OSU was relatively new to the game, entering its eighth season of organized play. And it showed. According to the student newspaper, *Michigan Daily*:

> Michigan had no trouble in defeating the Ohio State University representatives in Saturday's game. Two halves of 20 and 15 minutes, respectively, were played, and the score was 34–0. It was not so much Michigan's strength as Ohio's weakness that brought about the score. The visitors lined up with three of their best players absent, while Michigan put her best team on the field. While the form of the varsity team was not on the championship order, it showed an improvement over the Saturday before that was most encouraging.

Indeed, the Wolverines were coming off a scoreless tie from the previous week against that noted football power, Ohio Wesleyan.

Against the Buckeyes, it was no contest. Why the game was played with one half at 20 minutes and the second at 15 is beyond me, but perhaps it was better in this case. Michigan not only dominated, but actually had a 50-yard touchdown run called back on a penalty.

It should be noted that the *Michigan Daily* made mention that, "The entire team played gentlemanly and not a single wrangle arose to mar the game."

Good to know.

1902

OHIO STATE	0	0	0
MICHIGAN	45	41	86

This game came in the midst of the Fielding Yost coaching dynasty in an era known as the "Point-a-Minute" teams, and it could have been worse.

Obviously, this was the biggest blowout, the largest margin of victory for either team in the storied rivalry. And to think, if it wasn't for a new rule enacted by Stanford University that allowed only graduates to coach its football teams, Yost might never have made his way to Ann Arbor. But he did, and the rest is legendary, glorious history.

So, how does it get any worse than 86–0? Well, according to OSU historian Jack Park in a story written on bucknuts.com, "You have to remember that in some of those games, touchdowns were only worth four or five points, so it's really even worse than it sounds."

And the Ohio State game wasn't even the highest scoring game of the 1902 season for Michigan. The Wolverines beat Iowa 107–0 and slipped past Michigan State 119–0.

Oh, by the way, some interesting notes about the 1902 game as reported by the *Michigan Daily*. Some 6,000 people attended the contest, which seemed like a whopping crowd at the time, and 2,000 of them came up from Columbus via train. The paper noted that Michigan fans shouted: "What will we do?

What will we do? We'll rub it in to OSU! That's what we'll do!" Clearly, the banter back and forth between the fans has been enhanced since then.

Something else happened that most certainly sums up the values and modesty of the time as compared to today. During the game, an Ohio State player had his jersey completely torn off. Players from both teams formed a human screen around the player while he changed into a new jersey so nobody from the crowd could see him.

Finally, there was something of a silver lining that came out of an 86–0 loss for OSU—somebody wrote the godawful Ohio State "Carmen Ohio" on the train ride home to Columbus.

Tom Harmon (98), Michigan's All-America back, breaks loose for a long gain against Ohio State at Ann Arbor on November 26, 1939. Harmon's all-around play helped the Wolverines defeat the Buckeyes 21–14 that day and then 40–0 the next year.

1940

MICHIGAN	13	7	13	7	**40**
OHIO STATE	0	0	0	0	**0**

In the long and famous history of Michigan–Ohio State, there have been many incredible individual achievements. One of the first, and maybe still the greatest, was that of Tom Harmon.

Harmon was Everybody's All-American long before *Sports Illustrated* writer Frank Deford wrote his book of the same name, which was loosely based on former Louisiana State star Billy Cannon.

Harmon, the father of actor and *NCIS* star Mark Harmon, was Michigan's first Heisman Trophy winner. In 1940 he rushed for 852 yards, passed for 506 yards, and had 21 total touchdowns. His season was punctuated on November 23, 1940, against the Buckeyes at Ohio Stadium when he scored two rushing touchdowns, threw for two touchdown passes, rushed for 139 yards, passed for 151 yards, kicked four extra points, and intercepted three passes, including one he returned for a touchdown.

"Old 98" broke the all-time college scoring record held by the legendary Red Grange of Illinois.

"I saw Tom Harmon play, and he was no doubt a pure Heisman Trophy winner," former Michigan tackle Alvin Wistert said in the 2003 Pat Summerall–produced and –narrated documentary, *Rivalries: The History of Michigan–Ohio State.* "He did everything. He punted, he passed, he received kickoffs, he

received punts, he played both offense and defense.... He was a great football player and a great person."

Added Michigan All-America halfback Bob Chappuis in the same film: "Tom Harmon was my idol. He was a senior at Michigan when I was a senior in high school. He was probably the best all-around football player that I ever saw. He did the whole thing. And he was fast."

For his efforts in that 1940 game against the Buckeyes, Harmon not only clinched the Heisman Trophy but received something that, to this day, is extraordinary—a standing ovation from the Ohio State faithful at Ohio Stadium.

Perhaps it was for the amazing game or for the amazing career. In three games against Ohio State, Harmon accounted for 618 yards—238 more than OSU as a team.

1950

MICHIGAN	2	7	0	0	**9**
OHIO STATE	3	0	0	0	**3**

One of the most remembered games of the series, recalled less for the outcome or memorable plays—there weren't any—but instead for the simple fact that the game took place in one of the worst blizzards in Ohio history. It has come to be known as the Snow Bowl.

First, as much as we hate to say it, give Ohio State credit. The weather was truly awful—*dangerous* might actually be the better term—and since it was OSU's home game, the school

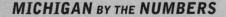
MICHIGAN *BY THE* NUMBERS

ALL-TIME RECORD VS. OHIO STATE: 57–44–6
BIGGEST MARGIN OF VICTORY VS. OHIO STATE:
   86 points (86–0), 1902
WORST DEFEAT VS. OHIO STATE: 38 points (38–0), 1935
LONGEST CONSECUTIVE WIN STREAK VS. OHIO STATE:
   Nine (1901–1909)
LONGEST CONSECUTIVE LOSING STREAK VS. OHIO STATE:
   Seven (2004–2010)
CONFERENCE TITLES: 42
HOME RECORD VS. OHIO STATE: 30–20–4
AWAY RECORD VS. OHIO STATE: 27–24–2
PF: 1,753
PA: 1,475

MICHIGAN

had the option of postponing the contest or even cancelling the game and retaining the Big Ten championship. OSU was ranked eighth in the country at the time; Michigan was unranked. Still, the winner was heading to the Rose Bowl.

To their credit, the Buckeyes decided to play—although Fritz Crisler's very clear admonition certainly had something to do with it. Crisler, then Michigan's athletics director, told his counterpart at OSU, "If we don't play today, I'm not coming back next week."

It was certainly nothing to write home about. The game, that is. The weather certainly was. The contest was played in near whiteout conditions with temperatures at 10 degrees at kick-off with a 29 mph wind, making it feel like 12 below zero.

The referees desperately tried to sweep and shovel snow off the yard lines, but the blizzard was relentless. It resulted in a whopping 45 punts between the two teams. Michigan didn't complete a pass, didn't gain a first down, and gained 27 yards on the day. Ohio State had three first downs and gained 41 yards.

Special teams proved to be the difference. Ohio State's Vic Janowicz, that year's eventual Heisman Trophy winner, kicked a 27-yard field goal to give the Buckeyes a 3–0 lead. But the Wolverines came back and blocked one of his punts that squibbed out of the end zone for a safety, trimming the deficit to 3–2.

Late in the second quarter, Ohio State coach Wes Fesler decided to punt on a third down. It wasn't unusual—the weather was so bad and field position was so key that both teams had actually punted on first down on occasion during the game. In fact, Michigan quick-kicked on the first play of the game.

But this particular decision to punt proved disastrous.

"I'm sitting up there because I'm kind of a redshirt guy and not dressed for the game," recalled former Ohio State player and coach Earle Bruce in the documentary *Rivalries: The History of Michigan–Ohio State*, "and I'm sitting behind a little old lady about 83 years old, and she jumps up and says, 'Don't you punt that ball, Fesler! Don't you dare punt that ball!' I jumped up and said, 'I'm with you, lady. Don't punt the ball!' We punted the ball. They blocked it. We lost the game 9–3, and Fesler never coached another game."

Of course, the game simply could not be remembered without having a classic Michigan–Ohio State twist attached to it. Brothers Robert and Tony Momsen were squaring off against each other in the game and, as fate would have it, both played pivotal roles.

Robert "Buckeye Bob" Momsen recovered a blocked Michigan punt early the game that set up Janowicz's field goal that gave OSU a 3–0 lead. But it was Michigan's Tony Momsen who scored the game's decisive, and only, touchdown, when he chased down the punt that the Wolverines blocked on OSU and fell on it in the end zone for the score.

1969

OHIO STATE	6	6	0	0	**12**
MICHIGAN	7	17	0	0	**24**

This is arguably the greatest game in the history of the rivalry.

The backstory—there's always a backstory with Michigan–Ohio State, right?—was what led to this not only being considered the greatest game of the rivalry but also one of the greatest games in college football history and, ultimately, a game that ABC television announcer Bill Flemming ended by saying, "There it is! What has to be the upset of the century!"

Ohio State came into the game as the defending national champion under Woody Hayes and with a 22-game winning streak. The Buckeyes were considered unbeatable. More importantly—and this can't be stated enough—just the year before, OSU had beaten Michigan 50–14—and, late in the

MICHIGAN

MICHIGAN'S MILESTONE VICTORIES

Win	Date	Opponent	Home/Away	Score
1	May 30, 1879	Racine	A	1–0
50	Nov. 29, 1894	Chicago	A	6–4
100	Oct. 5, 1901	Case	H	57–0
200	Oct. 9, 1915	Mt. Union	H	35–0
300	Oct. 1, 1932	Michigan St.	H	26–0
400	Oct. 23, 1948	Minnesota	A	27–14
500	Nov. 11, 1967	Illinois	A	21–14
600	Oct. 21, 1978	Wisconsin	A	42–0
700	Nov. 4, 1989	Purdue	H	42–27
750	Sept. 9, 1995	Memphis	H	24–7
800	Sept. 30, 2000	Wisconsin	H	13–10

game, Hayes made the decision to go for a two-point conversion with his team up by five touchdowns. When asked by reporters afterward why he went for two, Hayes replied, "Because I couldn't go for three."

It was also the first season of coaching at U-M for a former Hayes assistant who went on to make his mark as a head coach at Miami of Ohio, drawing the attention of the University of Michigan—Glenn E. "Bo" Schembechler.

And the new guy never let the Wolverines forget what happened the year before.

"When we went to our locker room to get our equipment, we saw the number '50' everywhere," former Michigan offensive

lineman Dick Caldarazzo said in the Michigan–Ohio State documentary. "Bo had put '50' on everything you could see. All the shower curtains were '50,' there was a '50' on everybody's locker."

"That stuck in the craw of the Michigan players," Schembechler said in the documentary. "You know, when you have an intense rivalry that's very close and one game gets out of hand and you rub it in like that, it'll come back to haunt you."

Legend has it that Schembechler told his players, "Get me through the first 30 minutes with a lead, and I'll beat the old man in the next 30 minutes."

And that's how it played out. All 36 points were scored in the first half. Ohio State drew first blood when it pinned Michigan deep in its own half of the field, got the ball back in good field position, and scored on a one-yard run by Jim Otis to take a 6–0 lead on a missed extra point.

The two teams traded scores on the next two possessions. Michigan went up 7–6, but the Buckeyes came right back and drove down the field to take a 12–7 lead (the Bucks kicked the PAT, but when Michigan was called offside, Hayes went for two and failed).

Then the key sequence. The Wolverines started the next possession at their own 33-yard line and methodically drove to OSU's 33. Schembechler called for a tailback draw, and Billy Taylor gained 28 yards on the play to set up a touchdown that put U-M ahead for good, 14–12.

Michigan held OSU to a three-and-out on the next possession, forcing a punt that Barry Pierson returned 60 yards to OSU's 3-yard line, setting up another score that made it 21–12.

After stopping Ohio State yet again, Michigan drove from its own 36 to OSU's 3-yard line again, settling for a field goal and the final points of the half—and the game.

Legendary broadcaster Bob Ufer said at the end of the broadcast, "Ripley couldn't have written it any better than this!"

"We played a tremendous game at Iowa the week before, and not many people realize that Iowa is not that bad a team," Schembechler said after the game. "In the locker room, we talked about beating Ohio State even before we took our uniforms off.… We took the field against Ohio State, and that was the most enthusiastic football team I've ever been associated with."

At a 40-year reunion of the game in 2009, Schembechler's widow, Cathy, said, "Of all the boys Bo coached, the '69 team was the one he was closest to and remained close to forever. He meant a lot to them, and they meant a lot to him."

1986

MICHIGAN	3	3	13	7	26
OHIO STATE	14	0	3	7	24

Call it the Jim Harbaugh Game. Fans remember this game for what was, at the time, a rather brash statement in the college

ranks—Harbaugh's guarantee that the Wolverines would beat the Buckeyes in their annual encounter.

Harbaugh made the statement in the aftermath of a shocking loss to Minnesota the week before, the team's first of the year, and he backed it up by going 19-of-29 for 261 yards against the Buckeyes.

But in reality, it became the Jamie Morris game.

Morris rushed for a career-high 210 yards—150 in the second half—and scored two touchdowns.

"You know, you have to go back to the week before," Morris recalled. "We went to Minnesota and got caught looking ahead to Ohio State. We watched film of Minnesota, but, you know, as young kids sometimes do, we saw it and thought that Minnesota wasn't that good and it would be easy. And we got beat."

It was something that head coach Bo Schembechler actually feared, Morris said.

"He saw how we had practiced before the Minnesota game and he said it in his pregame speech—'I hope this week doesn't hurt us,'" Morris recalled. "The funny thing that not many people know about that game is, this was going to be Bo's [166th] victory at Michigan, the most of any Michigan coach. So we got a plaque already, before the game, and we were going to present it to Bo. But we lost, so we had to scrape off the 'Minnesota' and put 'Ohio State' in there."

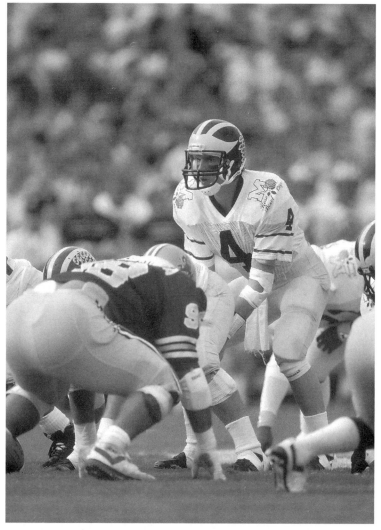

Michigan quarterback Jim Harbaugh guaranteed a victory against Ohio State in 1986, and his teammates followed through with a win. He led the team to the Rose Bowl that year, but couldn't keep the winning going, losing to Arizona State 22–15. Photo courtesy of Getty Images

When Michigan went into Columbus a week later, "We were all very quiet, very somber, very serious about the game," Morris said. "We had just lost our undefeated season and our No. 2 [national] ranking. We knew we were a better team than what we showed against Minnesota."

Morris said Schembechler came into his hotel room the night before the game and said, "I need you to visualize. I need you to see yourself doing good things with the ball." Morris paused and then laughed and said, "And, of course, we got down 14–3 right away."

Michigan was still down 17–13 when Morris took over. His 52-yard run set up his own eight-yard TD run to put U-M up 19–17 after a missed two-point conversion, and Morris had the bulk of the carries on an 85-yard drive that resulted in Thomas Wilcher's seven-yard score for a 26–17 advantage.

As for Harbaugh's bold prediction of victory, Morris said the team backed their senior quarterback 100 percent.

"As a player, you like to see your leader making a statement like that," Morris said. "He believed in that team. That was his senior year. He made a statement that we were going to win. Bo was pissed because it was bulletin-board material that would fire Ohio State up. In the pregame meeting, Bo said, 'Our quarterback shot his mouth off, so we have to go out there back it up.' He didn't like it, but we needed that kick in the pants. We needed Jim to say that."

1995

OHIO STATE	3	6	6	8	**23**
MICHIGAN	7	3	7	14	**31**

1996

MICHIGAN	0	0	10	3	**13**
OHIO STATE	3	6	0	0	**9**

These games are grouped together because, well, you can't love one without loving the other. And it marked the beginning of the end for Ohio State coach John Cooper.

In both seasons, Cooper took his Buckeyes into The Game with an undefeated record and a No. 2 national ranking. Any hopes of a national title in either season were dashed by the Wolverines. And, really, isn't that the best kind of victory? To beat a team so deliciously close to the pinnacle, only to pull them back at the last second and make their heartbreak even more maudlin? Yeah, it is.

The 1995 game was basically a one-man show, while the 1996 game was a collective effort on the part of the defense.

In 1995 it was all Tshimanga "Tim" Biakabutuka, who rushed for a whopping 313 yards—still a record for most individual rushing yards in a Michigan–Ohio State game—and the Wolverines beat the Buckeyes 31–23.

"I'm obviously disappointed," OSU coach John Cooper said after the game. "I don't know if I've ever been as disappointed in my life as I am right now."

Somebody should have warned him about the '96 game. Biak-abutuka broke off a 22-yard run on the game's first play and never looked back. Ohio State wide receiver Terry Glenn, who later would be aptly called "she" by head coach Bill Parcells when both were in the NFL with the New England Patriots, had guaranteed a victory earlier that week by saying the Buck-eyes would be playing in the Rose Bowl.

Let's put it this way: Glenn is no Jim Harbaugh.

His "guarantee" was as soft as he is. Glenn dropped two balls in the game that his own school newspaper described as "two passes that should have been routine catches," and instead it was Northwestern that ended up in its first Rose Bowl game in 46 years.

And, in a bit of Shakespearean foreshadow, a true freshman by the name of Charles Woodson intercepted two passes in the game.

A year later, in 1996, the Buckeyes came in with another jugger-naut team and expectations of playing for the national champi-onship. And for the better part of two-plus months, that's how it played out. OSU was unstoppable, or so it seemed. The Buck-eyes scored less than 27 points just once all season entering the Michigan game—a 17–14 win over Wisconsin—and twice rolled up 70 points. They were as good on the road as they were at home, scoring wins at No. 5 Notre Dame—yes, back when Notre Dame was good—at Purdue, and at No. 20 Iowa.

But, this was the Choker, er, Cooper Era, and as these cyclical things go—and, yes, your current winning streak *is* cyclical,

OSU fans—all of that went out the window when it came time to play The Game.

This time, two forces combined—Mother Nature and defense. U-M's defense, which was just coming into its own and would carry over into the national championship year of 1997, held the Buckeyes to just nine points. And Mother Nature provided a bit of a slippery field, or at least in one spot where All-America safety Shawn Springs fell down on a simple 10-yard pass from Brian Griese to Tai Streets, who bolted the last 59 yards to paydirt on the second play of the second half that catapulted Michigan to the victory.

At the time, the Wolverines trailed 9–0. That cut it to 9–7, and U-M added two second-half field goals while the defense held OSU to 84 total yards in the second half. Once again, the loss ended an unbeaten season for the Buckeyes and any shot at a national championship. At the time, neither the Big Ten nor the Pac-10 were part of the fledgling Bowl Alliance, and both its champions were obligated to play in the Rose Bowl, which OSU was still headed to.

"It's sickening, it's an awful feeling," Ohio State fullback Matt Calhoun said after the game. "I thought, *I can't have this type of feeling again*, and here I am feeling it again."

"We have had a good year, but it's not a great year when you don't beat Michigan," Cooper said.

Michigan safety Marcus Ray summed it up best when he said, "I'd rather not go to the Rose Bowl and beat Ohio State, than go to the Rose Bowl and not beat Ohio State."

1997

OHIO STATE	0	0	7	7	14
MICHIGAN	0	13	7	0	20

Ah, one of the ones we keep near and dear to our hearts.

This is the year where the tables were turned. It was Michigan this time that came into the game undefeated and ranked No. 1, and it was No. 4 OSU looking to spoil the season and prevent the Wolverines from going to the Rose Bowl and playing for the national championship.

The only difference, of course, is that Michigan doesn't choke.

The Wolverines took a 20–0 lead and held on for the six-point victory in a game that not only capped an undefeated season, but clinched the Heisman Trophy for Charles Woodson, who had a fabulous game in front of a national television audience.

Just three weeks after Woodson had another big game on national TV in the 34–8 win over Penn State that catapulted U-M into the No. 1 spot in the polls, Woodson—primarily a defensive player—caught a 37-yard pass that set up one score and ran back a 78-yard punt for a touchdown. He also intercepted a pass while performing his day job as one of the top lockdown cornerbacks in the country.

This was also the game that wide receiver David Boston failed to learn from history—OSU players just shouldn't be making any guarantees. Boston was quoted during the week leading up to the game, saying that he played against defensive backs

every day in practice who were better than Woodson and that the Buckeyes would win.

Boston did catch a long touchdown pass from Stanley Jackson, but for the most part was not a factor—and, in what became an iconic *Sports Illustrated* cover photo, Boston was shown being laid out in mid-air on a great hit by Michigan safety Marcus Ray.

"Charles Woodson is the greatest player I've ever been around," former Michigan coach Lloyd Carr said on the documentary *Rivalries: The History of Michigan–Ohio State.* "He made every single guy that was around him better. If his best friend wasn't working hard, Charles Woodson would not spare him."

1998

MICHIGAN	0	7	7	7	21
WASHINGTON STATE	7	0	6	3	16

A little more than a month after Michigan beat Ohio State in the '97 regular season finale, the Wolverines headed to Pasadena for the first day of 1998 to play Washington State in the Rose Bowl.

The Cougars were a surprise entry out of the Pac-10 and had a dynamic quarterback in Ryan Leaf.

But the Wolverines had a quiet quarterback in Brian Griese, and at the end of a checkered career, he saved his best for last. Griese, who was a walk-on and had to overcome an incident at a local Ann Arbor bar, decided to come back for a fifth season

and was outstanding, including the comeback win over Iowa that preserved Michigan's unbeaten season.

In the Rose Bowl, he would go 18-for-30 for 251 yards and three touchdowns to lead the Wolverines to the thrilling victory and a share of their first national championship in almost 50 years, since Bennie Oosterbaan's 1948 team posted a perfect 10–0 record.

The victory capped an amazing season for the Blue. The program entered the 1997 year with four consecutive four-loss seasons, and head coach Lloyd Carr was on the spot in his third year to deliver. Many had opined that the block M now stood for mediocrity, but with the convincing season-opening win against Colorado, the Wolverines carved their own path.

For Carr, ever the master motivator, it was a series of one-game seasons throughout 1997, as trite as that might sound. Carr saw that symbolism of overcoming the odds and had given every player an ice-climbing pick that year with their name etched in it. It was a reference to the best-selling book *Into Thin Air* by Jon Krakauer, about an ill-fated assault on Mount Everest.

Carr said the players bought into it immediately.

"The responsibility for that goes to our seniors," he said on his weekly television show, *Michigan Replay*, after the 1997 Ohio State win. "We had great senior leadership. Jon Jansen did a great job of that. Eric Mayes continued to be an instrumental leader on our team [after being injured against Indiana and missing the rest of the season]."

MICHIGAN

U-M BOWL RECORDS AND RANKINGS

COACH	BOWL (YEAR/RESULT)	FINAL RANKING
Yost	Rose (1901/W, 49–0 vs. Stanford)	
Crisler	Rose (1948/W, 49–0 vs. USC)	No. 1
Oosterbaan	Rose (1951/W, 14–6 vs. Cal)	No. 9
Elliott	Rose (1965/W, 34–7 vs. Oregon St.)	No. 4
Schembechler	Rose (1970/L, 10–3 vs. USC)	No. 9
Schembechler	Rose (1972/L, 13–12 vs. Stanford)	No. 6
Schembechler	Orange (1976/L, 14–6 vs. Oklahoma)	No. 8
Schembechler	Rose (1977/L, 14–6 vs. USC)	No. 3
Schembechler	Rose (1978/L, 27–20 vs. Washington)	No. 9
Schembechler	Rose (1979/L, 17–10 vs. USC)	No. 5
Schembechler	Gator (1979/L, 17–15 vs. N. Carolina)	No. 18
Schembechler	Rose (1981/W, 23–6 vs. Washington)	No. 4
Schembechler	Bluebonnet (1981/W, 33–14 vs. UCLA)	No. 12
Schembechler	Rose (1983/L, 24–14 vs. UCLA)	UR
Schembechler	Sugar (1984/L, 9–7 vs. Auburn)	No. 8
Schembechler	Holiday (1984/L, 24–17 vs. BYU)	UR
Schembechler	Fiesta (1986/W, 27–9 vs. Nebraska)	No. 2
Schembechler	Rose (1987/L, 22–15 vs. Arizona St.)	No. 8
Schembechler	Hall of Fame (1988/W, 28–24 vs. Ala.)	No. 19
Schembechler	Rose (1989/W, 22–14 vs. USC)	No. 4
Schembechler	Rose (1990/L, 17–10 vs. USC)	No. 7
Moeller	Gator (1991/W, 35–3 vs. Mississippi)	No. 7
Moeller	Rose (1992/L, 34–14 vs. Washington)	No. 6
Moeller	Rose (1993/W, 38–31 vs. Washington)	No. 5
Moeller	Hall of Fame (1994/W, 42–7 vs. NC St.)	No. 21

Moeller	Holiday (1994/W, 24–14 vs. Colo. St.)	No. 12
Carr	Alamo (1995/L, 22–20 vs. Texas A&M)	No. 17
Carr	Outback (1997, L 17–14 vs. Alabama)	No. 20
Carr	Rose (1998/W/21–16 vs. Wash. St.)	No. 1
Carr	Citrus (1999/W, 45–31 vs. Arkansas)	No. 12
Carr	Orange (2000/W, 35–34 [OT] vs. Ala.)	No. 5
Carr	Citrus (2001/W, 31–28 vs. Auburn)	No. 11
Carr	Citrus (2002/L, 45–17 vs. Tennessee)	No. 20
Carr	Outback (2003/W, 38–30 vs. Florida)	No. 9
Carr	Rose (2004/L, 28–14 vs. USC)	No. 6
Carr	Rose (2005/L, 38–37 vs. Texas)	No. 14
Carr	Alamo (2005/L, 32–28 vs. Nebraska)	UR
Carr	Rose (2007/L, 32–18 vs. USC)	No. 8
Carr	Capital One (2008/W, 41–35 vs. Fla.)	No. 18
Rodriguez	Gator (2011/L, 52–14 vs. Mississippi St.)	UR

MICHIGAN

The game is one that we love for obvious reasons—it was the first national championship at Michigan in nearly 50 years—and for other reasons, as well. If you were at the game, you couldn't help but get swept away with emotion. If you watched on TV, it was much of the same as ABC analyst Bob Griese broke down after his son was named the Rose Bowl's MVP.

"This is a dream. It's been a wonderful season.... We got something to celebrate now," Lloyd Carr said on ABC after the game.

It was the first and only time to date that Michigan finished 12–0.

In the cramped locker room at the Rose Bowl after the victory over the Cougars, Carr stood in the middle of his players and said, "You have left a wonderful legacy for every team that ever follows you. *You* just won the national championship."

2003

OHIO STATE	0	7	7	7	**21**
MICHIGAN	7	14	7	7	**35**

As we said before, Michigan doesn't choke in the big games. Especially at home.

This one, well, this one was as big as they come—the 100th game in the history of the storied rivalry.

Oh, and, uh, it's also the last game in the series that Michigan has won to date.

Moving on.

The 100th game in the history of the series naturally was accompanied by huge pomp and circumstance and media coverage. ABC announcer Keith Jackson did the voiceover for the intro to the game, and it was, of course, magnificent.

"This is a remarkable festival, annually, whether here or at the Horseshoe," Jackson said. "There are the great bands. 'Fight that team across the field, show 'em Ohio's here.'... 'Hail to

the victors valiant, hail to the conquering heroes.'... Today, another bounty of memories concluding a hundred years of Buckeyes and Wolverines."

Both quarterback John Navarre and tailback Chris Perry had big games. The former threw for 278 yards and two touchdowns, the latter rushed for 154 yards and scored twice against an Ohio State defense that was giving up an average of just 50.4 yards rushing per game.

And once again it was another season in which the loss denied Ohio State a likely chance to play in the national championship game. The Wolverines went on to the Rose Bowl—although even that looked iffy when U-M got off to a 4–2 start after losing to Oregon and Iowa. In fact, the Wolverines were looking at 4–3, as they were down 28–7 to Minnesota in the fourth quarter the week after losing to the Hawkeyes.

But Navarre rallied the team to a 38–35 victory, and Michigan was off to its first outright Big Ten championship and Rose Bowl in six years.

2
PLAYERS WE LOVE

IF THEY PUT ON THE WINGED HELMET and wore the maize and blue, it stands to reason that we love *all* Michigan football players. It takes someone special to strap on the gear and play football; it takes someone extraordinary to play for the greatest college program in the history of the sport.

Here are a few guys who just struck more of a chord with us (in no particular order).

TOM HARMON

This is all you need to know about Tommy Harmon—he once walked away from a plane crash.

One of the greatest, if not the greatest, Michigan football players in history, "Old 98" simply did it all. Though the Michigan game programs often listed Harmon as a halfback, he also played quarterback, receiver, place-kicker, and punter. Harmon played the full 60 minutes in eight games during his three-year career. He accumulated 3,438 yards rushing and passing during his time at U-M, and he won the Heisman Trophy and the Maxwell Award as a senior in 1940.

Harmon was drafted No. 1 overall by the Chicago Bears of the National Football League, but he instead opted to join the Army as a pilot. During World War II, his plane was shot down in combat, and Harmon walked away from the wreckage. Of course, he did.

Harmon later went on to a successful broadcasting career after marrying actress Elyse Knox, with whom he had three children—actress Kelly Harmon; actress Kristin Harmon Nelson, who married singer Ricky Nelson of *Ozzie and Harriett* fame; and son Mark Harmon, a former UCLA quarterback and now a successful actor in his own right.

His jersey is just one of five retired by the school, and he, Ron Kramer, and President Gerald Ford were the first three football players inducted into the University of Michigan Athletic Hall of Honor.

TOM BRADY

It's hard to believe now, but Tom Brady was once in a quarterback duel at Michigan with a kid named Drew Henson.

Henson was the Golden Child, a local kid from nearby Brighton, Michigan, who basically rewrote the national high school record book in football and baseball (breaking Bo Jackson's high school RBI mark, by the way).

Though Brady had that *something* that everybody could see, coach Lloyd Carr remained firm in his commitment to play Henson in a platoon situation. But even Carr could see into

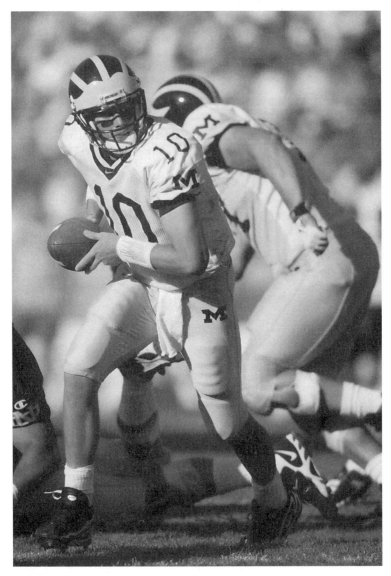

Quarterback Tom Brady went 1–1 against Ohio State, including the 1999 win that sent Michigan to the Orange Bowl, where the Wolverines won in overtime against Alabama.

the future what seemingly nobody else could see—this author will never forget Carr fielding question after question about the platoon system during Brady's junior year (Henson's freshman season) and at one point saying, "Look, don't worry about Tom Brady. Tom Brady's going to play in the NFL."

He sure did.

At Michigan, Brady went 1–1 against Ohio State. The 24–17 win in 1999 vaulted U-M into the Orange Bowl to play Alabama, where Brady was magnificent. He went 34-for-46 for 369 yards, four touchdowns, and no interceptions in a 35–34 overtime win over the Crimson Tide.

For his career, Brady finished with 5,351 yards in basically two-plus seasons, with 35 TD passes and a 62.3 completion percentage. He is a three-time Super Bowl champion with the New England Patriots.

JIM HARBAUGH

Jim Harbaugh guaranteed that Michigan would beat Ohio State in 1986. For that alone he has the undying love of U-M fans (although his comments about the school's academics and his decision to spurn his alma mater in 2011 and take the head coaching position with the San Francisco 49ers left a bad taste in the mouths of some).

Nonetheless, Harbaugh has to be on this list. He was a three-year starter for Bo Schembechler, though he broke his arm and missed the last six games of his sophomore year in 1984, including a 21–6 loss to Ohio State. Harbaugh came back

and beat OSU in 1985 and then, in 1986, after the unbeaten Wolverines were stunningly upset at Minnesota, Harbaugh said this: "I guarantee we will beat Ohio State and go to Pasadena."

In 2007 Harbaugh told *USA Today*, "The way our leader, Bo Schembechler, handled it was genius. He just came into the team meeting, and I'm kind of expecting to get an earful. He said, 'Well, at least I know our quarterback thinks we can win. Rally around him. Let's go to Columbus and beat the Buckeyes.'"

Michigan won 26–24.

Harbaugh led the nation in passing efficiency in 1985 in guiding the Wolverines to a 10–1–1 mark; in 1986 he was the Big Ten Player of the Year and third in the Heisman Trophy balloting after an 11–2 campaign.

CHARLES WOODSON

How good was Charles Woodson?

As a freshman, he intercepted two passes to ensure the 31–23 upset of Ohio State. By the time he was a junior, Woodson was so good that he cut off a third of the field on defense since opposing teams rarely, if ever, threw to his side.

Coach Lloyd Carr called him the greatest football player he's ever been around, and with good reason. Although Woodson was primarily a defensive player, he also returned punts and occasionally played receiver on offense.

And he became the first primarily defensive player to win the Heisman Trophy in 1997, based largely on his body of work, including three nationally televised plays that showcased all three of his talents. At Michigan State, Woodson made one of the greatest interceptions of all time when he leaped near the sideline and made a one-handed grab, and got a foot inbounds, in a tight 13–7 game against the Spartans that the Wolverines went on to win. Against Penn State, also on the road, Woodson broke free on the slot and caught a 37-yard touchdown pass from Brian Griese that led to the 34–8 blowout win that vaulted U-M from No. 4 to No. 1 in the polls. And against Ohio State in the regular season finale, Woodson returned a punt 78 yards for a touchdown in a 20–14 win over the Buckeyes that put the Wolverines into the Rose Bowl, where they ultimately beat Washington State for a share of the national championship.

ANTHONY CARTER

Many players have left a legacy at Michigan. Anthony Carter is No. 1.

Jersey No. 1, that is.

While it's hard to place into context the kind of heritage that people like Harmon, Crisler, Yost, Schembechler, Woodson, Brady, and all the great people involved with Michigan football over the years have left on the program, Carter's is tangible. His uniform number, No. 1, has become a legacy fixture among wide receivers at U-M. To receive the coveted No. 1 is a badge of honor to be worn proudly.

Carter had an amazing career at Michigan, becoming just the eighth three-time All-American in Big Ten Conference history—and the first in 36 years—when he earned the honor for the third time in 1982. He was twice a team MVP (1980 and 1982) and the Big Ten's MVP in his senior season in 1982.

Carter finished his career with 3,076 yards in receptions on 161 balls caught, 37 of which went for touchdowns. Surprisingly, Carter only went 1–3 against Ohio State during his career. But he might be best remembered for the last-second touchdown catch against Indiana in 1979, grabbing a ball over the middle from quarterback John Wangler, eluding three defenders and getting to the end zone as the gun sounded for a 27–21 victory.

RON KRAMER

Ron Kramer is a star in one of the great "hometown boy makes good" stories.

There have been many amazing athletes to come to the University of Michigan, but perhaps none as talented and versatile as Kramer, who hailed from East Detroit and had less than an hour's drive to campus for college.

Kramer was not only a tremendous football player, but in fact was a nine-time letterman during his career in Ann Arbor, winning three varsity letters each in football, basketball, and track.

He was twice an All-America end in football (1955 and '56) and was a 2,000-point scorer for the basketball team (1,119

points as a junior and 1,124 points as a senior, to be exact). His football jersey No. 87 was retired by the school. According to the University of Michigan's Bentley Library, on at least one occasion Kramer participated in spring football drills, walked over to the U-M track for a meet, and won the high jump with a leap of 6'4"—a tremendous feat for someone with a 230-pound football body.

Kramer went on to a successful career with both the Green Bay Packers and Detroit Lions in the NFL, and remains one of the most beloved Michigan players of all-time.

RICK LEACH

Like Ron Kramer, Rick Leach was a gifted and extraordinary athlete. And that's not hyperbole, either.

Leach was an All-American in football and baseball. He was a four-year starter from 1975 to 1978 for Bo Schembechler, a left-handed dream who could not only throw the ball but run it. He set a then–NCAA record for most touchdowns accounted for (82) and broke Big Ten records for total offense (6,460 yards), total plays (1,034), and touchdown passes (48).

At the beginning of his sophomore year, Leach ended up on the cover of *Sports Illustrated*'s college football preview issue. And there was no jinx—sophomore, cover boy, or any other. Beginning that season, Leach led Michigan to three consecutive wins over Ohio State and three straight trips to the Rose Bowl.

When it was all said and done, Leach was drafted as a senior by not one, not two, but three teams—the NFL's Denver

TOP PERFORMANCES vs. OHIO STATE

RUSHING: Tim Biakabatuka, 313 yards, 1995
PASSING: Tom Brady, 375 yards, 1998
RECEIVING YARDS: Braylon Edwards, 172 yards, 2004
RECEPTIONS: Marquise Walker, 15, 2001
MOST POINTS: Tom Harmon, 22, 1940
FIELD GOALS: Adam Finley, 2002; Jay Feeley, 1998; Ali Haji-Sheikh, 1981; David Allerdice, 1909, all tied with 3
LONGEST PUNT RETURN: Desmond Howard, 93 yards (TD), 1991
INTERCEPTIONS: Barry Pierson, 1969; Harry Kipke 1922, both with 3
TOTAL TACKLES: Tom Stincic, 23, 1968

MICHIGAN

Broncos, the Montreal Alouettes of the Canadian Football League, and baseball's Detroit Tigers.

He opted to pursue a career in baseball, playing 10 years for four different teams.

DESMOND HOWARD

The catch. And the punt return. Two plays that forever are burned in the memories of Michigan fans. They are bookend plays, really, one coming at the beginning of the season and the other at the end. They were enough to make the 1991 season a memorable 10–2 campaign that finished with a trip to the Rose Bowl. In large part, thanks to Howard.

The wide receiver won the Heisman Trophy that year by the second-largest margin of victory ever at the time. He caught 62

Michigan wide receiver Desmond Howard (21) strikes the "Heisman" pose moments after scoring on a 93-yard punt return in a 31–3 trouncing of Ohio State in 1991 at The Big House. Photo courtesy of Getty Images

balls for 985 yards and 19 touchdowns receiving that year, and also added a kickoff return for a touchdown and a punt return.

The best of his receptions came in the second game of the season. Clinging to a 17–14 lead against Notre Dame in the fourth quarter and facing a fourth-and-1 at their own 25-yard line, the Wolverines opted to surprise Notre Dame with a pass. Elvis Grbac's throw was just a tad long—but not so long that Howard couldn't dive, stretch out as far as he could like Superman, and haul in the pass for a stunning touchdown.

The punt return, of course, was as electric as it gets—93 yards to the house against Ohio State in a victory that clinched the Rose Bowl, and punctuated by the famous Heisman Trophy pose in the end zone.

Howard went on to win a Super Bowl MVP with the Green Bay Packers in 1997 and is currently a college football analyst with ESPN.

JAMIE MORRIS

The little engine that could. And did.

How can you not love Jamie Morris? At just 5′7″, Morris might have been small, but he was dynamic. Initially, coach Bo Schembechler didn't recognize that. When Morris arrived on campus for his freshman year in 1984, Bo recalled for the *New York Times* that, "I told Jamie when we recruited him he was too small to be a running back and we wanted him for running back kicks. I did, however, promise him the chance to try to be a running back for us. Good thing I did, isn't it?"

Good thing. Morris was inserted into the starting lineup as a tailback three games into his freshman season…and never came out. In his four-year career he became the first player to ever lead the Wolverines in rushing four straight seasons, a mark since tied by Mike Hart. He rushed for 1,703 yards in his senior season, the third-best all-time in U-M history.

A versatile player, Morris also caught 99 passes in his career for 756 yards and is fifth on the all-time school list for kickoff return yardage. He finished with 6,201 all-purpose yards. But Morris' best game came against—you guessed it—Ohio State during his junior year.

Morris ran for 210 yards, caught 22 yards worth of passes, and had 70 yards in kick returns for 302 all-purpose yards in Michigan's 26–24 victory.

DAN DIERDORF

C'mon now. How could a guy born in Canton, Ohio, *not* become a great football player? The home of the Pro Football Hall of Fame also produced one of the greatest offensive linemen in Michigan history in Dan Dierdorf.

The burly tackle was twice named All–Big Ten and was a consensus All-American in 1970. Michigan was 25–6 during the three years Dierdorf started for the Wolverines. He is a member of both the College Football Hall of Fame and the Pro Football Hall of Fame. During his career in the NFL, Dierdorf was part of the St. Louis Cardinals' famed offensive line that included Tom Banks, Roger Finnie, Bob Young, and Conrad Dobler. In 1975 the group collectively allowed just eight sacks

in 14 games. Individually, Dierdorf did not allow a sack for the entire 1976 and '77 seasons.

JON JANSEN

A true iron man of Michigan football.

One of the great offensive linemen in Michigan history, Jansen started 50 consecutive games at right tackle for the Wolverines, a school record. It's quite an achievement if you think about it. Like players before him who were known for their longevity (Rick Leach, Anthony Carter, Tom Harmon, etc.), Jansen needed a combination of factors to do it, including remaining injury free, being good enough to start as a freshman, and having the luxury of playing 12- and 13-game seasons that included an NCAA-allowed extra game and, of course, a bowl game.

A two-time team cocaptain, Jansen was the Big Ten Offensive Lineman of the Year in 1998 and was also named GTE/ CoSIDA Second-Team Academic All-America. He received Michigan's Big Ten Medal of Honor for his academic and athletic achievements.

Jansen is best known for being the rock that held Michigan's line together in the 1997 national championship season.

BOB CHAPPUIS

We've used the adjectives "amazing" and "tremendous" many times in this book, but it's hard to find a better, more apt description for Bob Chappuis.

MICHIGAN

WOLVERINES IN THE
COLLEGE FOOTBALL HALL OF FAME

NAME/YEARS AT U-M	POSITION	INDUCTION
Albert Benbrook/1908–1910	Guard	1971
David Brown/1972–1974	Defensive Back	2007
Lloyd Carr/1995–2007	Coach	2011
Anthony Carter/1979–1982	Wide Receiver	2001
Bob Chappuis/1942–1947	Halfback	1988
Fritz Crisler/1937–1947	Coach	1954
Tom Curtis/1967–1969	Defensive Back	2005
Dan Dierdorf/1967–1972	Tackle	2000
Bump Elliott/1946–1947	Halfback	1989
Pete Elliott/1945–1948	Quarterback	1994
Bennie Friedman/1923–1926	Quarterback	1951
Tom Harmon/1937–1940	Halfback	1954
Willie Heston/1901–1904	Halfback	1954
Elroy Hirsch/1943	Halfback	1974
Desmond Howard/1989–1991	Wide Receiver	2010
Ron Johnson/1965–1968	Halfback	1992
Harry Kipke/1920–1923	Halfback	1958
Ron Kramer/1953–1956	End	1978
George Little/1922–1924	Coach	1955
Jim Mandich/1966–1969	End	2005
John Maulbetsch/1914–1916	Halfback	1973
Reggie McKenzie/1968–1971	Guard	2002
William Morley/1895	Halfback	1971
Harry Newman/1931–1933	Quarterback	1954
Bennie Oosterbaan/1924–1927	End	1954

Merv Pregulman/1940–1943	Guard/Tackle	1982
Bo Schembechler/1969–1989	Coach	1993
Germany Schulz/1904–1908	Center	1951
Neil Snow/1898–1901	End/Fullback	1960
Ernie Vick/1917–1921	Center	1983
Bob Westfall/1938–1941	Fullback	1987
Elton "Tad" Weiman/1921–1928	Coach	1956
Albert Wistert/1938–1942	Tackle	1968
Alvin Wistert/1946–1949	Tackle	1981
Francis Wistert/1930–1933	Tackle	1967
Fielding Yost/1901–1924, '26	Coach	1951

MICHIGAN

Think about it. He began his University of Michigan career in 1942, played one season for the Wolverines, and then was drafted into the U.S. Army for World War II. He flew 21 missions as a radio operator and aerial gunner during his three-year stint in the service, and his plane was shot down in northern Italy on its 21st mission. Chappuis and two other crew members survived and were hidden by Italian resistance members for three months, until the war in Europe ended in May 1945.

Chappuis then returned to play football at Michigan and, despite missing three years off the field, simply excelled.

He led coach Fritz Crisler's 1947 Mad Magicians to a 10–0 record, including a win over Ohio State—another W over the

Buckeyes came in the '48 season, too—and a 49–0 win over USC in the Rose Bowl. Chappuis earned All-America honors as well as Rose Bowl MVP honors as the Wolverines captured the Associated Press national championship in a bit of a controversial selection over Notre Dame.

Chappuis was featured on the cover of *Time* magazine that year as well in an article titled "The Specialist," which talked about Crisler's decision to specialize the offensive and defensive units at U-M. At a time when virtually every player went both ways, playing offense and defense, Crisler separated the two squads into 11 different players on each side of the ball.

Chappuis briefly played professional football in the All-America Football Conference in 1948 and 1949, but instead of jumping to the NFL, he retired when the AAFC folded. He is a member of the College Football Hall of Fame.

HARRY KIPKE

Harry Kipke was truly Mr. Michigan. He played at U-M. He coached at U-M. He was a regent for the university. He was involved with anything that had even a remote hint of maize and blue.

Like Ron Kramer, Kipke was a nine-time letter=winner while at Michigan—three in football, three in basketball, and three in baseball. He was an All-American in football in 1922 and widely considered to be the best punter of his time and one of the best in school history. During his three-year career, Kipke helped Michigan to a 19–1–2 record, a 2–1 record against Ohio State from 1921 to 1923, and the 1923 national championship.

As a coach, Kipke led the Wolverines for nine seasons and went 46–26–4, including a pair of back-to-back national championships in 1932 and '33. Along with Fielding Yost—for whom he played—and Bo Schembechler, Kipke is one of just three men to have coached Michigan teams to four consecutive conference championships.

ALVIN, FRANCIS, AND ALBERT WISTERT

Ah, the Wistert brothers. How cool is this story?

The three grew up in Chicago, and in the late 1920s a friend of Francis "Whitey" Wistert was invited to visit the University of Michigan. Francis tagged along for the trip and, like most people who visit Ann Arbor and the campus, was thoroughly impressed and mesmerized by the school's beauty.

Really, it's not like he visited OSU on the banks of the dirty Olentangy, where he would have likely done an about-face and enrolled at Northwestern or Illinois. No, Francis loved the place and came to Michigan in the fall of 1929. He was soon followed by his brothers. And all three made history.

"If I'm not mistaken, I think this is unprecedented in the annals of college football: that three brothers all would go to the same school, all played football. All played tackle, all wore the same No. 11, all made All-American. Two of us played on four national championship teams. And all were inducted into the College Football Hall of Fame," Alvin Wistert told the *Detroit News* for a 2004 article.

Unprecedented and totally cool.

TSHIMANGA BIAKABUTUKA

Meet Tshimanga "Just call me Tim" Biakabutuka. He will for-ever live in Michigan lore for his performance in the 1995 game against Ohio State, rushing for 313 yards in a stunning 31–23 upset of the Buckeyes. But that was a just a piece of his over-all body of work that year—he still holds the program's single-season rushing record with 1,818 yards.

Biakabutuka was drafted No. 8 overall by the Carolina Pan-thers in 1995, but his short six-year stay in the league was injury-plagued.

In 2010, in an interview with annarbor.com, Biakabutuka recalled his time at Michigan.

"You look back in college and you remember the fun and you remember the camaraderie, a bunch of little kids with little money in their pockets playing hard for each other and still have that friendship," he said. "When I went back to the golf tournament, some of the guys you play with, it just reminds you how much of a good time that part of your life comes with. For everybody, I'm sure, college is the best time of your life. Even in the pros, college was that time, the best time of my life. So I'm very, very happy to have it as a Wolverine."

ROB LYTLE

Sadly, Lytle passed away on November 21, 2010, at the age of 56. He is remembered as the great player he was—an All-America running back at Michigan who had a stel-lar career for the maize and blue and went on to score a

touchdown in the Super Bowl in 1978 as a rookie with the Denver Broncos.

"He was one of the toughest guys I ever played with and one of the best leaders, who made the ultimate sacrifice for us by playing fullback at times," former teammate Rick Leach told the Associated Press after Lytle's death.

Lytle was the Big Ten's MVP and an All-American in 1976 when he finished third in the Heisman Trophy balloting behind Pitt's Tony Dorsett and Southern Cal's Ricky Bell. Lytle rushed for a total of 3,317 yards and 26 touchdowns in four seasons, from 1973 to 1976. The 1976 team beat Ohio State and went to the Rose Bowl.

"Rob was a teammate and an incredibly terrific guy," Michigan athletics director David Brandon said in a statement. "It's a sad day because we've lost someone who was a great example of a Michigan man."

JON RUNYAN

Hey, that's Congressman Runyan to you, Ohio State fans. Runyan was an All–Big Ten offensive lineman for Michigan in 1995, wrapping up a stellar career that included 34 starts and two victories in three years over Ohio State. He was a 1996 fourth-round draft pick of the Houston Oilers, and went on to play 14 years in the NFL before turning his attention to politics.

In 2010 he ran for New Jersey's Third Congressional District seat and ousted Rep. John Adler in the race, assuming his place in the House of Representatives.

MICHIGAN

U-M PLAYERS CURRENTLY IN THE NFL

PLAYER	TEAM	POSITION
Adams, Jamar	Philadelphia Eagles	Safety
Arrington, Adrian	New Orleans Saints	Wide Receiver
Avant, Jason	Philadelphia Eagles	Wide Receiver
Baas, David	San Francisco 49ers	Guard
Backus, Jeff	Detroit Lions	Off. Tackle
Brady, Tom	New England Patriots	Quarterback
Branch, Alan	Arizona Cardinals	Def. Tackle
Breaston, Steve	Arizona Cardinals	Wide Receiver
Brown, Stevie	Oakland Raiders	Safety
Brown, Carlos	New York Jets	Running Back
Burgess, Prescott	Baltimore Ravens	Linebacker
Butler, Carson	New England Patriots	Tight End
Collins, Todd	Chicago Bears	Quarterback
Edwards, Braylon	New York Jets	Wide Receiver
Feely, Jay	Arizona Cardinals	Place-kicker
Foote, Larry	Pittsburgh Steelers	Linebacker
Goodwin, Jonathan	New Orleans Saints	Center
Graham, Brandon	Philadelphia Eagles	Defensive End
Hall, James	St. Louis Rams	Defensive End
Hall, Leon	Cincinnati Bengals	Cornerback
Harris, David	New York Jets	Linebacker
Hart, Mike	Indianapolis Colts	Running Back
Henne, Chad	Miami Dolphins	Quarterback
Hutchinson, Steve	Minnesota Vikings	Guard
Jackson, Marlin	Philadelphia Eagles	Safety

Jamison, Tim	Houston Texans	Defensive End
Jones, Dhani	Cincinnati Bengals	Linebacker
Long, Jake	Miami Dolphins	Off. Tackle
Manningham, Mario	New York Giants	Wide Receiver
Mathews, Greg	St. Louis Rams	Wide Receiver
Mesko, Zoltan	New England Patriots	Punter
Minor, Brandon	Denver Broncos	Running Back
Trent, Morgan	Cincinnati Bengals	Cornerback
Warren, Donovan	Pittsburgh Steelers	Safety
Watson, Gabe	Arizona Cardinals	Def. Tackle
Woodley, LaMarr	Pittsburgh Steelers	Linebacker
Woods, Pierre	Buffalo Bills	Linebacker
Woodson, Charles	Green Bay Packers	Cornerback

MICHIGAN

Like a true Michigan man, Runyan has been a board member for the Alzheimer's Association of South Jersey, and five times has hosted the Score for the Cure golf tournament, which benefits prostate cancer research.

BRIAN GRIESE

At the end of the 1998 Rose Bowl, after Michigan beat Washington State to clinch a perfect 12–0 season, there was the looming question of whether it would be the Wolverines or the Nebraska Cornhuskers who deserved the national championship.

Michigan quarterback Brian Griese stood in the interview room and was asked about that very scenario. He said, "I don't know what more we can do. I ask you, what more can we do?"

Nothing. Not a thing.

Griese will forever be remembered as the quarterback who delivered the school's first national title in almost 50 years when the Wolverines were named Associated Press national champions for their unbeaten 12–0 1997 season.

Griese, a walk-on who eventually earned a scholarship, had a brilliant campaign, completing 62.9 percent of his 307 passes that year for 2,293 yards, with 17 touchdowns and just six interceptions. He capped it with a 251-yard, three-touchdown performance against the Cougars in the Rose Bowl.

TYRONE WHEATLEY

Tyrone Wheatley was three-time All–Big Ten selection and ranks fourth on the Michigan career rushing yards record list with 4,178 yards. He also scored 47 touchdowns, good for second on the career list. Wheatley still holds the Michigan single-season yards-per-carry record (7.34 in 1992). His U-M teams were 2–1–1 against Ohio State from 1991 through 1994, though his 1994 senior season was marred by a shoulder injury that made him less than 100 percent.

Wheatley was drafted by the New York Giants and played 10 years in the NFL. He completed his first year as the running backs coach for Syracuse University in 2010.

BENNIE OOSTERBAAN

One of the all-time greats, Oosterbaan was a three-sport star who excelled at football, basketball, and baseball. Now, how do you define "excel"? Well, consider this. Oosterbaan was Michigan's first three-time All-American in football who led the Big Ten in scoring his senior season in 1927, including the dedication game of Michigan Stadium, when he threw three touchdown passes against Ohio State. He was also the Big Ten basketball scoring leader in the 1927–1928 season, earning All-America honors, and in the spring led the Big Ten in batting while playing baseball—a sport he didn't even play in high school.

Oosterbaan, of course, went on to coach at Michigan and led the 1948 team to an unbeaten record and the national championship—the last national title in football at U-M for 49 years until Lloyd Carr won the national crown in 1997.

During his 11 years as coach, Oosterbaan went 66–33–4, and Michigan won three Big Ten championships and the 1951 Rose Bowl. Oosterbaan also was the athletics director at Michigan.

MICHIGAN

MICHIGAN'S ALL-AMERICANS

One hundred twenty-six individual players have earned first-team All-America honors, representing 150 separate citations, including two three-time winners and 18 two-time All-Americans.

CENTERS

William Cunningham, 1898
Adolph "Germany" Schulz, 1907
Henry Vick, 1921
Jack Blott, 1923
Robert Brown, 1925
Maynard Morrsion, 1931
Charles Bernard, 1932, 1933
Walt Downing, 1977
George Lilja, 1980
Tom Dixon, 1983
John Vitale, 1988
Rod Payne, 1996
David Baas, 2004

TACKLES

Miller Pontius, 1913
Tom Edwards, 1925
Otto Pommerening, 1928
Francis Wistert, 1933
Albert Wistert, 1942
Mervin Pregulman, 1943
Alvin Wistert, 1948, 1949

Allen Wahl, 1949, 1950
Arthur Walker, 1954
William Yearby, 1964, 1965
Dan Dierdorf, 1970
Paul Seymour, 1972
Dave Gallagher (D), 1973
Bill Dufek, 1976
Curtis Greer (D), 1979
Ed Muransky, 1981
William Bubba Paris, 1981
Mike Hammerstein (D), 1985
John Elliott, 1986, 1987
Mark Messner (D), 1987, 1988
Greg Skrepenak, 1990, 1991
Chris Hutchinson (D), 1992
Jason Horn (D), 1995
John Runyan, 1995
Will Carr (D), 1996
Glen Steele (D), 1997
Jon Jansen, 1998
Rob Renes (D), 1999
Jake Long, 2006, 2007

GUARDS

Albert Benbrook, 1909, 1910
Ernest Allmendinger, 1917
Frank Culver, 1917
Edliff Slaughter, 1924
Harry Hawkins, 1925
Ralph Heikkenen, 1938
Julius Franks, 1942
Henry Hill, 1970
Reggie McKenzie, 1971

Mark Donahue 1976, 1977
Kurt Becker, 1981
Stefan Humphries, 1983
Dean Dingman, 1990
Matt Elliott, 1991
Joe Cocozzo, 1992
Steve Hutchinson, 1999, 2000

ENDS

Neil Snow, 1901
Stanfield Wells, 1910
Paul Goebel, 1922
Bennie Oosterbaan, 1925, 1926, 1927
Ted Petoskey, 1932, 1933
Edward Frutig, 1940
Elmer Madar, 1946
Richard Rifenburg, 1948
Lowell Perry, 1951
Ron Kramer, 1955, 1956
Jack Clancy, 1966
Jim Mandich, 1969
Jim Smith, 1976
Anthony Carter, 1980, 1981, 1982
Desmond Howard, 1991
Derrick Alexander, 1992
Jerame Tuman, 1997
David Terrell, 2000
Marquise Walker, 2001
Bennie Joppru, 2002
Braylon Edwards, 2004
LaMarr Woodley, (D) 2006
(D=Defensive end)

LINEBACKERS

Marty Huff, 1970
Mike Taylor, 1971
Calvin O'Neal, 1976
John Anderson, 1977
Ron Simpkins, 1979
Erick Anderson, 1991
Jarrett Irons, 1996
Larry Foote, 2001

HALFBACKS

Willie Heston, 1903, 1904
James Craig, 1913
John Maulbetsch, 1914
Harry Kipke, 1922
Tom Harmon, 1939, 1940
Robert Chappuis, 1947
Chalmers Elliott, 1947
James Pace, 1957
Richard Volk (D), 1966
Ron Johnson, 1968
Tom Curtis (D), 1969
Billy Taylor, 1971
Thom Darden (D), 1971
Randy Logan (D), 1972
Dave Brown, (D)1973, 1974
Don Dufek, (D), 1975
Rob Lytle, 1976
Butch Woolfolk, 1981
Brad Cochran (D), 1985
Garland Rivers (D), 1986
Tripp Welborne (D), 1989, 1990
Ty Law (D), 1994

Charles Woodson (D), 1996, 1997
Marlin Jackson (D), 2002, 2004
Chris Perry, 2003
Ernest Shazor (D), 2004
Leon Hall (D), 2006
(D=defensive halfback)

FULLBACKS
Cedric Smith, 1917
Frank Steketee, 1918
Robert Westfall, 1941
William Daley, 1943

QUARTERBACKS
Bennie Friedman, 1925, 1926
Harry Newman, 1932
Pete Elliott, 1948
Robert Timberlake, 1964
Rick Leach, 1978
Jim Harbaugh, 1986

KICKERS
Remy Hamilton, 1994

3

TRADITIONS WE LOVE

ONE OF THE REASONS there are so many college football fans is because of the great traditions, the pomp and circumstance, the tailgating, the camaraderie among students and alums, and the overall feel of a festive day. Saturday afternoons aren't just a game; they're an event.

And that's certainly the way it is in Ann Arbor, Michigan.

The history of Michigan football dates back more than 130 years, and as you might expect, there have been some great traditions built up over that time.

GO BLUE BANNER

Clemson has its rock, Florida State has its burning spear, Oklahoma has its Sooner Schooner. Michigan has its banner.

Although the tradition is relatively new, introduced in 1962, the 30-foot-long, five-foot-high blue banner with the maize lettering that spells out "GO BLUE" in capital letters (and "M Club Supports You" underneath) is one of the most recognizable traditions and game-day entrances in college football.

Michigan players jump to touch the Go Blue banner before a game, a winning tradition since 1962.

The Wolverines gather in the tunnel on the east side of Michigan Stadium, bunching together like a herd of wild horses waiting to be sprung free, and then make a mad dash for midfield, where they run under the banner, reaching up to touch it as they head toward the home sideline.

The 2011 season marks the 50th year of the tradition, and there are a couple of different, yet intertwined, origins of how it all came about. According to the school's official website, mgoblue.com, "Though the Graduate 'M' Club made the

permanent banner, it was the Undergraduate Club that started the tradition with a simple yellow block 'M' on a six-foot-wide strip of fabric. On the Friday practice before the 1962 team's homecoming game against Illinois, the 'M' Club assembled all the non-football letter-winners to form two lines as the players ran off the field toward the locker rooms in Yost Field House. The club was given permission by then-coach Bump Elliott to form the flag tunnel before the game the next day, and the rest is history."

But when the Michigan fan blog called "Those Who Stay Will Be Champions" recounted the origins of the banner back in 2007 on its site, Judy Renfrew Hart, daughter of former Michigan hockey coach Al Renfrew, responded with a comment of clarification:

> Just so you know, the tradition was started by Al Renfrew and Marguerite Renfrew. Marge was asked by Al to make two flags to drape over the Yost football locker rooms to cheer on the team. She made two flags, with a neighbor, Mrs. Helmers. The Block "M" was designed by Bob Hoisington, an engineering dean, to make sure it was correct. They hand-made the flags, which was not an easy feat at the time. They had the "M" Club members hang them over the Yost locker room to begin with, later it was moved to the tunnel at the stadium. After the games, they came back... and were hung at their house. Later it was changed to a banner. Al still [has] one of the original flags, with the football on the top of the flagpole.

The Go Blue banner quickly became ingrained as a Michigan fixture, both in the hearts of U-M fans and in the minds of

the opposition. Twice the banner has been stolen, and in 1973 Ohio State infamously came out of the tunnel at Michigan Stadium and tore down the banner. As Joel Pennington recalled in his book *The Ten-Year War: Ten Classic Games Between Bo and Woody*, normally the Buckeyes would come out of their tunnel and turn left to gather in front of their own sideline. But OSU player John Hicks went straight toward midfield, and the Buckeyes pulled down the banner being held by Michigan students and began jumping up and down on it. They quickly dispersed, but the classless incident left legendary Michigan radio voice Bob Ufer in a tizzy:

> Here they come: Hare, Middleton, and the Buckeyes and… they're tearing down Michigan's coveted M Club banner! They will meet a dastardly fate here for that! There isn't a Michigan Man who wouldn't like to go out and scalp those Buckeyes right now. They had the *audacity*, the *unmitigated gall*, to tear down the coveted "M" that Michigan's going to run out from under!… But the M-men will prevail because they're getting the banner back up again. And here they [the Michigan team] come! The maize and blue! Take it away, 105,000 fans!

Instead of running straight out through midfield under the banner, when Michigan took the field the Wolverines broke right and amassed in a group huddle in front of OSU's sideline before heading to their own sideline, back underneath the banner that had been quickly raised again.

Alas, the histrionics and emotions on both sides went for naught—the 1973 game ended in a 10–10 tie.

MICHIGAN'S BEST TRADITION: WINNING

How successful has the University of Michigan football program been? Let us count the wins, er, ways.

- *More all-time wins than any other Division I-A school (884)*
- *Leads the Big Ten with 42 league championships*
- *126 All-America first-team award winners*
- *Named national champions 11 times, including 1997*
- *National attendance leader 35 of the last 36 seasons*
- *231 consecutive Michigan Stadium home games with crowds in excess of 100,000*
- *First college-owned football stadium to seat more than 100,000*
- *The Wolverines have been ranked in the final Associated Press Top 25 poll in 37 of the last 42 seasons*

MICHIGAN

01

Michigan Stadium has undergone several renovations in the last decade or so, including the installation of the infamous and much-derided "halo" that ringed the stadium in the late 1990s (and lasted only two seasons); the installation of video scoreboards, also in the late 1990s; and a renovation of the stadium to install a new press box on the west side and premium seating on the east side of the facility that was completed in time for the 2010 season.

But every time they fix up the old girl and have to remove, or add, some seating, there is one constant. Capacity at Michigan Stadium will always end in "01." That's a nod to former athletics

director and football coach Fritz Crisler, who was AD in 1956 when Michigan Stadium was expanded to its 101,001 capacity. The "01" has traditionally been the honorary seat for Crisler.

THOSE WHO STAY WILL BE CHAMPIONS

It's more than just a sign on a wall or a coach's mantra. It's a creed. It's a belief. It's dogma. It's a way of life.

When Bo Schembechler was hired to coach the University of Michigan football team, the memory of a 50–14 humiliation by Ohio State in the 1968 game was fresh in everybody's mind. But so too was the fact that the Wolverines had won just one Big Ten championship between 1951 and 1968, that coming in 1964. That was an 18-year stretch that was hard to digest for U-M fans, especially with Ohio State and Woody Hayes competing for—and winning—Big Ten titles and national championships. So when legendary athletics director Don Canham went looking for a new coach to replace Bump Elliott, he focused squarely on Schembechler, who was enjoying success at Miami of Ohio.

When Schembechler took over, he had a sign placed in the training room: Those Who Stay Will Be Champions. Little did any of the players know what was in store for them. If the ESPN-produced movie *The Junction Boys* captured the difficulties of the Texas A&M training camp in the searing Texas heat under coach Bear Bryant, well, the winter and spring of 1969 in Ann Arbor, Michigan, weren't far behind.

In George Cantor's book, *I Remember Bo...*, offensive lineman Dick Caldarazzo, said of Schembechler, "He beat the crap out

of us those first few months of 1969. The walk-ons were dropping like flies. We had to run a mile in under six minutes, jump the stadium stairs on one leg, then jump upstairs on one leg with a teammate on your back. We hated it, and we hated him."

Dave Rentschler, who played at Michigan in the mid-1950s, became friendly with Schembechler from his days as a former M Club president. He told Cantor for the book that there was a method behind Schembechler's madness.

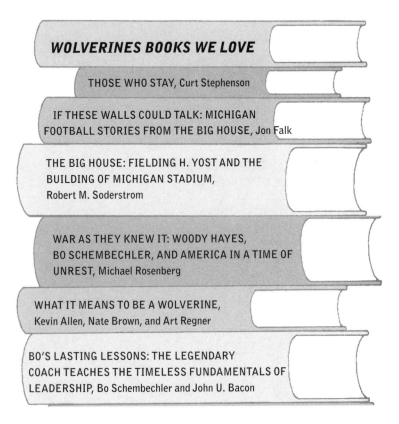

WOLVERINES BOOKS WE LOVE

THOSE WHO STAY, Curt Stephenson

IF THESE WALLS COULD TALK: MICHIGAN FOOTBALL STORIES FROM THE BIG HOUSE, Jon Falk

THE BIG HOUSE: FIELDING H. YOST AND THE BUILDING OF MICHIGAN STADIUM, Robert M. Soderstrom

WAR AS THEY KNEW IT: WOODY HAYES, BO SCHEMBECHLER, AND AMERICA IN A TIME OF UNREST, Michael Rosenberg

WHAT IT MEANS TO BE A WOLVERINE, Kevin Allen, Nate Brown, and Art Regner

BO'S LASTING LESSONS: THE LEGENDARY COACH TEACHES THE TIMELESS FUNDAMENTALS OF LEADERSHIP, Bo Schembechler and John U. Bacon

"These were someone else's players," Rentschler said. "Bo didn't recruit them. He had to find out in a hurry whom he could count on and whom he could trust. He set out to make sure the others left. That's why he put up the famous sign: 'Those Who Stay Will Be Champions.' Everyone who ever played for Bo always remembers that sign."

The Wolverines started with about 140 players at the beginning of winter workouts and spring ball. By the time the team reconvened that summer to begin training camp in preparation for the season, the roster was down to roughly 80 players. Or, to be exact, 80 survivors.

Cantor himself wrote that Schembechler was anathema to the times, and therefore to the players. Remember, this was 1969—Vietnam, the counterculture movement—and Ann

ALL-TIME NCAA DIVISION I-A WINS

School	Wins
Michigan	884
Texas	850
Notre Dame	846
Nebraska	836
Ohio State	829

Arbor and the University of Michigan campus were at the center of the Midwest's portion of the firestorm.

Not for Schembechler, though.

"In an era when we were all being told to do our own thing, whatever that was supposed to mean, and when anyone who advocated a disciplined life was regarded as a fascist, here was this guy who refused to bend," Cantor wrote, "who was uncompromising in his belief that doing things the tough way was the only right way."

Thomas Takach, a 1969 letter-winner and champion who stayed, said that players were leaving the program left and right.

"One afternoon between classes during spring practice, I decided to come in early in order to have my ankles taped for practice later that same day," Takach recalled for a 2009 article on the school's website commemorating the 40-year anniversary of the 1969 Big Ten champs. "As I arrived in the old football training room–locker room complex—which were adjacent areas on the second floor of Yost Field House—I found that the locker room was dark and completely deserted except for one person, John Prusiecki, a big defensive lineman from Indiana. He had just quit, and after informing the coaches of his decision had come in to clean out his locker. Failing to realize that he was not alone, he had taken a sharpie pen and below the words 'Those Who Stay Will Be Champions' on Bo's sign had added "and those who leave will be doctors, lawyers, and scientists." Eventually, most of the team saw the graffiti before the sign was replaced.

MICHIGAN

BEST. BAND. EVER.

The band? Well, now you're talkin'.

The Ohio State University marching band erroneously refers to itself as The Best Damn Band in the Land, an unfortunate self-satisfying, self-gratifying moniker that is as far removed from the truth as such other proclamations as "I will find the real killer" and "I did not have sex with that woman."

No, the greatest college band in America lives 185 miles north of Columbus, Ohio, in Ann Arbor—the Michigan Marching Band.

Here's all you need to know about the two marching bands. You know how Ohio State makes a big deal out of the Script Ohio and dotting of the "i"? We taught it to them.

Yep. True story.

Just like we taught Notre Dame how to play football, the Michigan Marching Band first performed a script "Ohio" during the 1932 Michigan–Ohio State game. Four years later, the OSU band first performed the Script Ohio. Oh, the OSU fans love to split hairs and say that when the MMB first did it, it was a set piece—that is, it wasn't formed through a march of the band members, as Script Ohio is formed now. But that's just semantics. The "best damn band in the land" knows it got its damn signature formation from the University of Michigan.

Besides, it's pretty easy to dot an "i" by just walking a few steps and...standing there. You want to impress us?

Cross a "t."

Or, better yet, try a back bend.

After the MMB pours onto the field from the tunnel at Michigan Stadium before every home game, it forms the signature Michigan logo, the block M, and then performs what is known as the "M Fanfare." This is a compilation of "The Victors," "Varsity," and "The Yellow and Blue."

At the climax of the song, the MMB drum major moves through the middle of the band toward the north end zone, or the student section, and stops at the 20-yard line. He or she then turns back to face the band, and as the "M Fanfare" reaches its final note, the drum major removes his or her hat and bends backward, like a gymnast, to touch their head to the ground.

Try pulling that one off, "i" dotters.

MICHIGAN

"That sign stating 'Those Who Stay Will Be Champions' remained in the locker room throughout spring practice, individual summer workouts, and the entire fall football season," Takach continued. "It became a primary, philosophical, motivating force for that team during the 1969 championship season and for future teams, as well, summarizing the driving force and encompassing the goals of the entire group of athletes who wear the maize and blue. As usual, it turned out that Bo was right—those who stayed did become champions.

We were the 1969 Big Ten football champions and the Big Ten representative in the Rose Bowl on January 1, 1970."

Caldarazzo said he finally realized what the mantra meant in the '69 win over Ohio State. "We controlled the game in the second half," he said. "I thought back to all those stupid conditioning drills and realized this is what it was all for. They couldn't keep up with us."

At the memorial at Michigan Stadium following Schembechler's death in 2006, Dan Dierdorf recalled the famous saying and found its deeper meaning.

"Those of us in 1969, we were the first people that ever heard that phrase here in Ann Arbor," the former U-M lineman said. "When Bo said, 'Those who stay will be champions,' that phrase really means that if you stayed with Bo, you would be a champion—not just when you were wearing the helmet of the Michigan Wolverines, but you would be a champion for the rest of your life."

GOLF COURSE TAILGATING

Across the street from Michigan Stadium is the gorgeous, yet unforgiving, Michigan golf course. Normally, it's the setting for four hours of playing one of the great college courses. But on select Saturdays during the fall, it hosts several hundred cars and thousands of Michigan football fans on its fairways.

While there are spots within spitting distance of the stadium that have great tailgating, including the Crisler Arena parking

lot which sits just behind the east side of the stadium, the golf course is the place to be.

For a noon game, the gates open at 8:00 AM. It's best to enter from State Street, cross the first fairway, and park on the ninth fairway. It's a great time and a great atmosphere, especially if you're into a more sophisticated tailgate as opposed to the drunken frat brothers routine.

The only downside? You have to exit the golf course two hours after the conclusion of the game, which doesn't leave a heck of a lot of time to savor the victory. But, then again, if you play your cards right for a 3:30 PM start, you'd be able to eat three meals on the course!

And the Michigan Golf Course isn't the only place to park. Adjacent to the college course is the nine-hole Ann Arbor Golf & Outing Club, which is also a cool place to tailgate. It holds more than 1,500 cars at $40 a pop.

Or, if you know somebody who knows somebody who knows somebody, you can always park in somebody's driveway or on their lawn. Remember, Michigan Stadium looks like it was picked it up and dropped into the middle of a residential neighborhood in Ann Arbor. While some homeowners clearly enjoy their privacy, others are practitioners of the great American pastime of capitalism. Some charge $50, $60, even upward of $100 to park on their driveway and/or lawn, and some have longstanding, yearly customers who are more than willing to pay the steep price for the privilege of walking across the street to Michigan Stadium.

One homeowner, who shall remain nameless, gets $50 a car and is able to park eight cars a game on his property.

"You do the math," he said. "That's $400 a game times six to eight games a year. That pays for my vacation."

THE WINGED HELMET

The winged helmet is *the* symbol of Michigan football, even greater perhaps than the block "M." Back in the day, virtually every school wore the same kind of headgear, usually a black or brown leather helmet. As the game progressed and the helmets became more advanced for safety, they nonetheless bore a resemblance to each other.

But when Fritz Crisler arrived at Michigan from Princeton in 1938, his sense of style and design came with him.

Michigan's winged helmet is the greatest, most recognized helmet in all of college football.

"Michigan had a plain black helmet, and we wanted to dress it up a little," Crisler recalled in a long-ago interview recorded by the U-M Bentley Historical Library. "We added some color [maize and blue] and used the same basic helmet I had designed at Princeton."

Ah, but it was more than that. Crisler also believed that the helmet design would make it easier for Michigan quarterbacks to spot Wolverine receivers down the field.

"There was a tendency to use different-colored helmets just for receivers in those days, but I always thought that would be as helpful for the defense as for the offense," Crisler said.

And he was right. According to the school's website, from the 1937 to 1938 seasons, Michigan nearly doubled its passing yards, cut its interceptions almost in half, improved its completion percentage, and went from 4–4 in 1937 to 6–1–1 in 1938.

Now, the winged helmet is not only used by the Michigan football team, but by the U-M hockey team, catchers for the baseball and softball teams, field hockey goalies, and even the swim team's racing caps.

But the greatest thing about the winged helmet? It's the perfect symbol of the team, the team, and the team. Unlike that school down south, Michigan doesn't need to reward players by giving them stickers of what look like marijuana plants— fitting for Ohio State, though—to plaster on the back of the helmet.

THE VICTORS WALK

At press time, it was unknown whether new Michigan coach Brady Hoke would incorporate much from the Rich Rodriguez regime, but one of the traditions the new coach will hopefully keep is the Victors Walk.

This wasn't Rodriguez's baby; a version of the Victors Walk had been instituted by coach Bump Elliott in the 1960s and kept up by Bo Schembechler for a few years after he took over in 1969, but RichRod brought it back in 2008.

SINGING "THE VICTORS"

The most famous fight song in the country, "The Victors," was written by Louis Elbel, a U-M student, in the fall of 1898. He wrote it as a celebration of Michigan's 12–11 victory over then-archrival University of Chicago.

The Victors was first played publicly by none other than the great John Philip Sousa in the spring of 1899. Sousa called it "the best college march ever written."

And, of course, he was right.

> *Hail! to the victors valiant*
> *Hail! to the conqu'ring heroes*
> *Hail! Hail! to Michigan,*
> *the leaders and best*
> *Hail! to the victors valiant*
> *Hail! to the conqu'ring heroes*
> *Hail! Hail! to Michigan*
> *the champions of the West.*

While not as elaborate as the Grove at Ole Miss, the Victors Walk is a 200-yard walk by the Michigan football players from the east side of Crisler Arena, through the parking lot and the cheering fans and tailgaters, to the locker room entrance at Michigan Stadium.

NO. 1 JERSEY

Arguably, the No. 1 jersey is the most coveted uniform number in Michigan football.

While six players wore the No. 1 from 1919 to 1978, the jersey was made most famous and most popular by three-time All-America wide receiver Anthony Carter, who wore it during his career from 1979 to 1982.

Since then, it had been reserved for a wide receiver and had become something of a privilege to be given the No. 1 jersey—and with it, an acknowledgment of a certain level of talent and an expectation that the recipient would live up to its lofty status.

The No. 1 jersey is so important in Michigan lore that it actually ignited a public firestorm when Rich Rodriguez was the U-M coach. During the off-season of 2008, Rodriguez gave the No. 1 jersey to incoming freshman defensive back J.T. Floyd of Greenville, South Carolina. This upset former Wolverines wide receiver Braylon Edwards, who wore the No. 1 at U-M and who had endowed a generous $500,000 scholarship to the athletic department for the Michigan player worthy of wearing the No. 1 jersey.

PLAYERS WHO HAVE WORN NO. *1* AT U-M

PLAYER	POSITION	YEARS WORN
Angus G. Goetz	LT	1919–1920
Robert Jerome Dunne	G	1921
Paul G. Goebel	E	1922
Harry Kipke	HB	1923
Dave Whiteford	DB	1973–1975
Gregg Willner	PK/P	1976–1978
Anthony Carter	WR	1979–1982
Greg McMurtry	WR	1986–1989
Derrick Alexander	WR	1990–1993
Tyrone Butterfield	WR	1994–1996
David Terrell	WR	1998–2000
Braylon Edwards	WR	2003–2004

Edwards was so upset that he went public in May 2008, telling ESPN's Mike Tirico (an Ann Arbor resident) on Tirico's radio show: "I'm glad you gave me a Go Blue question because RichRod gave the No. 1 jersey to an incoming freshman DB, and the No. 1 jersey has never been worn by anybody outside of a wide receiver. It dates back to Anthony Carter, [Greg] McMurtry, Tyrone Butterfield, Derrick Alexander, David Terrell, and yours truly. So I'm going to have a talk with him about that the next time I see him. He's getting that call soon—very soon. Exactly, we have a jersey scholarship fund for this whole deal. What is he thinking?"

The disagreement was eventually sorted out, although Rodriguez probably didn't do himself any favors when he admitted

he did not know the history and tradition of the No. 1 jersey, nor did he know of Edwards' scholarship endowment. The former coach switched Floyd's jersey to No. 12, but Edwards still harbored resentment. In a January 2010 game between his New York Jets and the Cincinnati Bengals on NBC's *Sunday Night Football*, Edwards introduced himself as "Braylon Edwards, [from] Lloyd Carr's University of Michigan."

4

COACHES WE LOVE

THE UNIVERSITY OF MICHIGAN FOOTBALL program has been blessed with a plethora of outstanding coaches. Entering their 132nd year of football in 2011, the Wolverines have had 18 coaches, and only two of them have had losing records. Five of them have combined to win the program's 11 national championships. One of them had the vision, the foresight, the chutzpah, and the marketing savvy to convince the Board of regents to build a new stadium—a stadium in which the 84,000 seats could easily be expanded to 100,000 or more. Yet one man stood above all others.

GLENN E. "BO" SCHEMBECHLER

"What the mind can conceive, the mind can achieve, and those who stay will be champions."

How does one properly describe the man who never won a national championship at Michigan, was 2–8 in the Rose Bowl and 5–12 overall in bowl games in his 21-year career?

The answer is simple.

He revived, and then defined, Michigan football.

Bo Schembechler is carried on the shoulders of his players after the Wolverines defeated USC 22–14 in the 1989 Rose Bowl. That game is just one of the many reasons we love him.

Bo Schembechler—the "Bo" came from his sister, who had trouble pronouncing "brother" when she was young—was hired after the 1968 season and the 50–14 debacle against

Ohio State. It wasn't so much that game as it was the preceeding two decades—one Rose Bowl appearance since 1951.

He played football at Miami of Ohio under Woody Hayes and was a Hayes assistant for five years at Ohio State. Of course, people like Schembechler and Charles Woodson and numerous other Ohioans long to escape the dreariness of the state, which is why they head north to Michigan.

And that's where Schembechler wound up after being hired by athletics director Don Canham.

"Dick Larkins was the athletics director at Ohio State at the time, and he said, 'Oh, Bo, don't hire that guy. Don't hire that guy. You're going to end up just like I do with Woody. He's the same kind of guy,'" Canham said in the 2003 documentary *Rivalries: The History of Michigan vs. Ohio State.* "And I said, 'Well, I might be looking for the same kind of guy.'"

> *"When your team is winning, be ready to be tough, because winning can make you soft; on the other hand, when your team is losing, stick by them. Keep believing."*

Here's a classic Bo story.

In December 1996 I was hired by the *Ann Arbor News* to cover the Michigan basketball program and to serve as the columnist on Michigan football. My editor at the time, Geoff Larcom, always encouraged me to set up lunches and meet-and-greets with Michigan officials who didn't necessarily have the title of "coach" or "athletics director." It was always good to know as many people as possible, he said, a practice that proved to

be most beneficial when the Ed Martin scandal engulfed the men's basketball program soon thereafter.

Larcom also told me to set up a meeting with Bo Schembechler. Even if it wasn't for a story or on the record, it would be good for me to get to know Bo. After all, he still maintained an office in the building that bore his name, Schembechler Hall, not far from then-coach Lloyd Carr.

For nine months during that off-season, I tried in vain to set up a meeting. Nada. On occasion, we would end up in the same place—Crisler Arena, Yost Ice Arena, somewhere in the football offices—and I barely received a grunt from him.

During the 1997 football season, former athletics director Don Canham revived the practice of the Friday Night Smoker, which was basically nothing more than an informal cocktail party attended by members of the Michigan athletic department and football program, members of that week's opposing team's athletic department and football program, media members, and some other selected guests.

My wife and I attended the first of these, and as we walked in we saw Bo with his second wife, Cathy, a lovely woman whom he met in Florida. Bo had lost his first wife, Millie, to cancer, and Cathy was a godsend to him.

After my wife spotted him, she turned to me and said, "Still not talking to you, is he?" When I said no, my wife—a Brooklyn-born redhead—said, "I'll take care of this." I said to her, "Babe, don't. That's *Bo Schembechler*. I'll handle it." To which she

replied, "What's the difference who he is? He puts his pants on the same as everybody else."

She introduced herself to Bo, and the next thing I know, I was watching from afar as the two of them had what appeared to be a fun, engaging conversation. She then came toward me with Bo, arm in arm, and he extended his hand and said, "Bo Schembechler." I shook it, laughed, and said, "Rich Thomaselli." He said, "I know who you are." So I seized the opportunity and said, "Coach, I know you've gotten the messages from your secretary. I've been here nine months, and you haven't said a word to me. My wife introduces herself, and you two chat it up for 20 minutes. What gives?"

And Bo said, "Son, there's two reasons for that. One, she's far prettier than you. Two, I just realized in 20 minutes that she knows more about football than I've seen in your writing in nine months."

That was Bo.

> *"I love to win. Love it. Football is just too hard and too tough if you're not successful. This isn't just recreation, and the sport isn't for everybody. I just don't want to expend all this time and effort and come up short."*

Bo Schembechler loved the game of football.

"He told me many times, 'Football should be played in the afternoons,'" recalled Jim Brandstatter, who played under Bo, served as the cohost of his weekly television program *Michigan*

Replay, and also served as the master of ceremonies at Schembechler's memorial at Michigan Stadium after Bo passed in November 2006. "He would not stand for a 3:30 start or an 8:00 start. Therefore, ladies and gentlemen, toe meets leather at 1:14 exactly."

What Bo loved best about football was trench warfare. In many respects, that's what made Bo a bit of a clone of his mentor, Woody Hayes. The two of them shared the same philosophy—there's only three things that can happen when you throw the football, and two of them are bad. Thusly, the three-yards-and-a-cloud-of-dust mentality that would pervade and characterize Big Ten football for decades.

So it's no surprise, really, that his 21 seasons at Michigan featured 25 All-Americans—nine from the offensive line and 13 on defense.

The only thing Bo Schembechler loved more than football in general was the University of Michigan in particular. After he retired from coaching in 1989, and after brief stints as the school's athletics director and then as president of the Detroit Tigers, he raised millions for U-M Hospital, including cancer research in his first wife's name, and gave countless speeches that invoked his time at Michigan. According to the brilliant book by John Bacon, *Bo's Lasting Lessons: The Legendary Coach Teaches the Timeless Fundamentals of Leadership*, Schembechler had a voracious appetite for knowledge. He even audited a class on politics at the Gerald Ford School of Public Policy, where he constantly told his much younger classmates to remove their baseball hats while out in public.

But that was Bo.

"If I make a mistake, I'm going to make a mistake aggressively and I'm going to make it quickly. I don't believe in sleeping on a decision."

No, Bo didn't win any national championships. But he won or shared 13 Big Ten Conference championships and, more importantly, restored the pride and the luster to the Michigan football name.

Schembechler remains Michigan's winningest coach, with 194 victories in 21 seasons. He preached toughness—his 1969 winter, spring, and preseason training camp regimens are legendary among the survivors of his first season of coaching— and yet he did it with such conviction and confidence that his players would willingly and blindly follow him into battle.

But in large part, that was because he himself had a devotion to his players that was unequivocal. Schembechler died on a Friday, November 17, 2006, the day before one of the most historic meetings ever between Michigan and Ohio State—a matchup of the No. 1 Buckeyes and No. 2 Wolverines, both undefeated. On the Tuesday after the game, a memorial service was held at Michigan Stadium that drew hundreds of his former players and coaches, as well as 15,000 fans.

Then-coach Lloyd Carr, a longtime assistant under Schembechler, recalled being called off the road while recruiting in the early 1980s to attend an emergency, mandatory meeting at Schembechler's home of the entire coaching staff.

Schembechler told the staff he had been approached by Texas A&M University to take over their football program. He was offered a salary that would have made him the highest-paid coach in college football at the time.

Carr said the staff discussed the move and admitted that half the coaches wanted to stay in Ann Arbor, but that half wanted to go to Texas A&M.

"At the end of the meeting, with a tear in his eye and a crack in his voice, he said, 'Yes, but you don't have to tell those players you're leaving,'" Carr said.

Schembechler stayed. Why? Well, because those who stay will be champions.

"I am going to treat you all the same. Like dogs."

Bo used to call Jamie Morris the dumbest American in America, a phrase he would repeat to many of the Michigan players who went through Ann Arbor. Morris wasn't the only lucky one.

By the time those players were sophomores and juniors, they became accustomed to his trantrums. By the time they graduated, they wore them as a badge of honor.

And not just the players, either.

In his hilarious book, *If These Walls Could Talk: Michigan Football Stories from the Big House*, former Wolverines equipment manager Jon Falk recounted his first day of work at U-M

in 1974. He was wearing a red jacket with the Miami of Ohio name and logo, and headed to Schembechler's office to introduce himself.

Schembechler wasn't impressed.

QUOTES WE LOVE

"I was like a father out there, chastising his son for talking to the wrong people." —Michigan defensive back Charles Woodson on Ohio State receiver David Boston's comments prior to the 1997 game, which Michigan won 20–14

"I guarantee we will beat Ohio State and go to Pasadena." —Michigan quarterback Jim Harbaugh before the 1986 game. Michigan won 26–24 and went to the Rose Bowl.

"If you could play the greatest game of your life, you would play it that day." —Michigan running back Rob Lytle, on the rivalry against Ohio State

"Damn you, Bo. You'll never win a bigger game." —Woody Hayes to Bo Schembechler after the 1969 game when the Wolverines upset the Buckeyes and ruined their undefeated season

"Those who stay will be champions." —Bo Schembechler

"What are you doing in my office with a red jacket on!" Schembechler screamed. "Nobody wears a red jacket in my office! You get out of here and don't came back until you have a blue jacket that says Michigan Football on it! I won't talk to you until you're wearing a blue Michigan jacket! Now get out!"

Falk quickly hustled down to the equipment room, talked somebody into giving him a jacket, and reappeared in Schembechler's office.

It was like night and day.

"Now that's better!" said Schembechler, smiling and extending a hand to Falk. "Welcome to Michigan!"

At the memorial service, Michigan great Reggie McKenzie recalled a similar story when Schembechler showed both his angry side and his brilliant, wry sense of humor.

Michigan played Missouri in a game where a blocked punt by the Tigers decided the contest. McKenzie said another Michigan great, Jim Mandich, had missed the block that allowed the punt to be blocked. Bo was furious, of course. Special teams, if anything, is as much a mental battle as it is physical. And Bo wasn't about to lose the mental edge in a game.

So on the first practice on Tuesday after the game, Schembechler had the team practice punt protection.

"Bo tells all the freshmen, 'Any one of you sons of bitches blocks a kick, I'll give you $20,'" McKenzie recalled, and sure enough the Wolverines' first team had a punt blocked.

"We're downfield, and all we hear is, 'You! You!' and Bo's running down the field at [Jim] Brandstatter," McKenzie said. "And he must have learned from Bobby Knight or something because he started clubbing [Brandstatter]. And Brandstatter is stopped and is like, 'What's going on?' And all of a sudden [an assistant coach] is in the back, screaming, 'Bo! Bo! It wasn't his fault. It wasn't Brandstatter!' And Bo looked at Brandstatter and said, 'Ah well, you needed it anyway.'"

They laughed. They all laughed, of course, because they knew the football Bo and the real Bo.

"He had an incredible will, an incredible will to win, to live, and to make a difference," Lloyd Carr said at the memorial service.

Added Dan Dierdorf: "We will be those good husbands and good fathers and all those things, Bo, you wanted us to be. We stayed. We are champions, and it's all because of you."

> *"Football is the American game that typifies the old American spirit. It's physical. It's hard work. It's aggressive. It's kind of a swashbuckling American sport. Football is not going to die. It is our American heritage."*

LLOYD CARR

> *"By your own soul, learn to live.*
> *If some men force you, take no heed.*
> *If some men hate you, have no care.*
> *Sing your song, dream your dreams*
> *Hope your hopes, and pray your prayers."*

This was the poem Carr recited when he announced his retirement at a press conference after the 2007 regular season had concluded. It tells you everything you need to know about the coach.

Carr was the most cerebral coach I ever met. He kept a mammoth dictionary on a pedestal outside his office door and made his players look up a new word and tell him about it every time they came to see him.

I have a soft spot for Lloyd Carr—perhaps because he was the one Michigan football coach that I covered as a reporter—and would hope that all Michigan fans feel the same. And, of course, he won a national championship, something Gary Moeller, Bo Schembechler, and Bump Elliott couldn't do before him.

In some ways, I found Carr to be the reluctant head coach. He always said he had the greatest job in the world as an assistant coach at Michigan, first for 10 years under Schembechler and then for five years under Gary Moeller. But in May 1995, in a matter of days, Carr went from comfortable assistant to uncomfortable head coach. Moeller had a few too many drinks at the now-defunct Excalibur restaurant in Southfield, Michigan, and then had a run-in with police while resisting arrest. When audiotapes of his tirade were played from coast to coast, there was no choice but to have him resign.

Athletics director Joe Roberson named Carr, then the defensive coordinator, the interim head coach. It was a difficult position for Carr, taking over for his friend. At the time, Carr

said, "I can't tell you what a terrible experience it was to see this proud man defeated. But he's tough. He will rebound."

Moeller did rebound. And so did Carr. He grew into the role of head coach, winning his debut game that fall of 1995 by coming back from a 17–0 deficit to beat Virginia 18–17. He had the interim tag lifted in November of that year. His first two seasons he led 9–4 and 8–4 campaigns, but his third year at the helm produced the 12–0 national championship season.

I also liked Carr for the same reason that most U-M fans revere Bo Schembechler—he was fiercely loyal to the University of Michigan and to his players.

"The coach-player relationship can be a strained one," Carr told annarbor.com in February of 2010. "I always tell the guys that, one day, we'll be friends. They don't believe me until they leave campus and we reconnect."

Like Bo, Carr helped raise millions for charity, specifically for Mott's Children's Hospital. In retirement, he served as an associate athletics director at U-M until 2010, doing a variety of fund-raising and awareness-raising, all in the name of Michigan.

FIELDING YOST

Fielding Yost was a man ahead of his time. Way ahead.

Not only did his innovation extend to the football field during his 25 years as the head coach, but his vision of the future of college athletics was unparalleled. On the field, he was

Fielding Yost (right), with Boss Weeks (left, with football) and Willie Heston (below), two members of his 1902 national championship team, which outscored its opponents 644–12, including the 86–0 whupping of OSU.

a genius. Some 90 years before football coaches start talking about their offense being a "fast break on turf," Yost was doing it. Starting with his first club in 1901, Yost's squads were known as the "Point-a-Minute" teams because, well, they literally scored a point a minute. From 1901 to 1905, Michigan went 56 consecutive games without losing, by a cumulative score of 2,821 to 42, an average score of 50–1. Included in that streak were national championships in 1901, 1902, 1903, and 1904.

Yost had two separate stints as coach, from 1901 to 1923 and 1925 to 1926. But from 1921 to 1941, Yost also served as the school's athletics director, and his impact might have been even greater off the field. Look around the Michigan campus, especially the athletic campus down on State Street. Everything you see comes from Yost's foresight. According to U-M's Bentley Library, among the projects constructed under Yost's direction were Michigan Stadium, the university's 18-hole golf course, the nation's first intramural sports building, and the nation's first multipurpose field house—now known as Yost Ice Arena.

About the only vision and foresight they have at Ohio State is picking the person to make the next beer run.

HARRY KIPKE

Kipke is in a select group among Michigan coaches, joining only Fielding Yost and Bo Schembechler in leading teams to four consecutive conference championships. That happened during the 1930 through 1933 seasons, when Kipke's Wolverines won four Big Ten titles and two national championships (1932 and 1933). During that span, Michigan went 34–1–3.

Kipke was one of the first men, at any college, to make the successful transition from former player to coach. During his playing days at U-M, Kipke was one of the great kickers in the country and was named as an All-America halfback. He was the school's first-ever winner of nine letters (three each in football, baseball, and basketball).

HERBERT O. "FRITZ" CRISLER

How's this for pedigree? Fritz Crisler graduated as an honors student from the University of Chicago; is one of only two players to earn nine letters in three sports at the school in football, basketball, and baseball; and played football for coach Amos Alonzo Stagg, considered one of the fathers of American football.

In 10 seasons, from 1938 to 1947, Crisler went 71–16–3 with a pair of Big Ten championships and a national championship after beating USC 49–0 in the 1948 Rose Bowl.

Like Yost, Crisler was also a visionary. When he came to Michigan from Princeton, he brought with him a design for the Wolverines' helmet that would help distinguish players downfield and allow the quarterback to better see his teammates. That design became the iconic winged helmet that is emulated and envied throughout college football.

BRADY HOKE

He hasn't done a thing yet. As of press time, he hasn't even won a game at Michigan. But on January 11, 2011, Brady Hoke was named as the 19th head coach in the 131-year history of Michigan football. Let's face it, after Lloyd Carr retired, the three-year tenure of Rich Rodriguez was among the most tumultuous in Michigan history. And, as far as wins and losses, it also happened to be the worst three-year stretch in the program's history. Hoke represents hope, and if that sounds a little bit like it did back in 1969, well…

The difference here between Schembechler and Hoke is that Hoke is already a Michigan man. Hoke spent eight seasons in Ann Arbor before embarking on his head coaching career at Ball State and San Diego State. As the defensive line coach, he guided three linemen to All-America honors during his tenure—William Carr (1996), Glen Steele, (1997) and Rob Renes (1999)—and had five players earn first-team All–Big Ten accolades.

A member of Michigan's staff during its 1997 national championship season, Hoke helped the defense lead the nation in rushing defense at 89 yards per game and 2.7 yards per carry. Michigan's team posted 5–3 records against Michigan State, Ohio State, and in bowl games during Hoke's tenure on the staff.

He knows Michigan tradition, and he knows Ohio State. And, like that cantankerous bully of a coach they used to have down at that school down south, Hoke refuses to refer to Ohio State.

"I think that rivalry is special, it's like none other in football," Hoke said at his introductory press conference. "Being engaged in that battle for eight years and growing up in the state, you knew Bo and Woody and the great fights they had. It is the most important game on the schedule. Not that the others aren't important, but it is the most important game on that schedule."

Granted, the U-M community had been mixed about hiring a coach with a 47–50 overall record in eight years at two smaller

MICHIGAN

MICHIGAN COACHING RECORDS

Coach	Years	vs. OSU	Overall
(None)	1879–1890	0–0	23–10–1
Frank Crawford	1891	0–0	4–5
Frank E. Barbour	1892–1893	0–0	14–8
William McCauley	1894–1895	0–0	17–2–1
William D. Ward	1896	0–0	9–1
Gustave Ferbert	1897–1899	1–0	24–3–1
Biff Lee	1900	0–0–1	7–2–1
Fielding H. Yost	1901–1923, 1925–1926	16–3–1	165–29–10
George Little	1924	1–0	6–2
Elton E. Wieman	1927–1928	1–1	9–6–1
Harry Kipke	1929–1937	3–6	46–26–4
Fritz Crisler	1938–1947	7–2–1	71–16–3
Bennie Oosterbaan	1948–1958	5–5–1	63–33–4
Bump Elliott	1959–1968	3–7	51–42–2
Bo Schembechler	1969–1989	11–9–1	198–48–5
Gary Moeller	1990–1994	3–1–1	44–13–4
Lloyd Carr	1995–2007	6–7	121–40
Rich Rodriguez	2008–2010	0–3	15–21

schools, but Hoke has been nothing but a combination of combustible energy and intense charm since being named coach. And, let's be honest, it's more than just about wins and losses and Xs and Os. Hoke represents a bridge to Michigan's past, having served as an assistant under Gary Moeller and Lloyd

Carr, and his hiring satisfies the requirement that wasn't met when Rodriguez was hired—he's a Michigan Man.

"I'm excited for Brady Hoke and even more excited for Michigan," said Michigan's 1997 Heisman Trophy winner, Charles Woodson, in a statement. "I'm glad this process is over and we can begin to restore the tradition and respect that was once Michigan."

"He is a man of integrity. He is one of the finest people I've ever dealt with. He was like a father figure to me when I was at school and after graduation," said former U-M lineman and current St. Louis Rams defensive end James Hall. "I stayed close to Brady, and I really got to know his family. He is a hard-working coach and has always expressed his love for Michigan football and the success of this program."

JOHN COOPER

My goodness, how can we *not* include Ohio State coach John Cooper among the coaches we love?

When Earle Bruce was fired as the Buckeyes' head coach in 1987, the school looked west to Arizona State, a program that had just gone to the Rose Bowl under head coach John Cooper.

In large part, Bruce was fired because he set a high bar in his first season that he could never live up to. After taking over following the Woody Hayes punching debacle, Bruce guided OSU to an 11–1 mark in 1979, losing the Rose Bowl—and possibly a piece of the national championship—by just a point, 17–16, to USC.

But Bruce then had six consecutive 9–3 seasons, a 10–3 mark in 1986, and then slumped to 6–4–1 in 1987 and was told he was out the week of the Michigan game. His inspired players responded with an upset win over the Wolverines, not only saving him from a .500 season but also saving him from a losing record against Michigan. As it was, Bruce went 5–4 in nine years against Michigan. If OSU fans thought that was bad, they had no idea what they were in store for when Cooper arrived from Arizona State.

John Cooper coached at Ohio State from 1988 to 2000, posting a record of 111–43–4. Ten of those losses—nearly a quarter—were to Michigan. Cooper went 2–10–1 against the Wolverines, and was 3–8 in bowl games. He never won an outright Big Ten title, though his teams did share three conference championships.

It wasn't just that Cooper lost to Michigan, it was the way he lost. His critics felt that Cooper coached "scared" in those games, coaching not to lose rather than to win, thus playing more conservatively against the Wolverines than he did the entire season.

Whatever the reason, the bottom line is that John Cooper was awful against U-M and in the postseason. Three times (1993, 1995, and 1996) Cooper's teams went into The Game undefeated and ranked among the nation's top five, and each time the Buckeyes lost to the Wolverines. Six times in his 11 years, Cooper ended the season with back-to-back losses to Michigan in the regular season finale and then in a bowl game. His undoing came in 2000 when OSU lost to unranked South Carolina—a team coming off an 0–11 campaign the

John Cooper may not have been a Michigan Man, but he did so much for the U-M football program, going 2–10–1 against the Wolverines as head coach of Ohio State from 1988 to 2001.

year before—24–7 in the Outback Bowl. He was fired a day later by then–athletics director Andy Geiger.

"It did not hinge on winning or losing the Outback Bowl, although I would say that yesterday was sort of a capstone on what we have seen as a deteriorating climate within the football program," Geiger said at the time. "Concern about discipline, competitiveness, academic pursuits, a whole series of things. I thought yesterday, unfortunately, was an exhibit of all those things rolled into one."

Indeed, it was a difficult final season for Cooper. Prior to the Outback Bowl, one player was booted from the team for

having a John Blutarsky–like 0.0 grade-point average; team MVP and leading rusher Jonathan Wells was held out of the starting lineup for missing the first practice in Tampa; and one offensive lineman sued another for $50,000 in the aftermath of an on-field fight.

One of the reasons Ohio State officials hired Cooper was Arizona State's 22–15 win over Michigan in the 1987 Rose Bowl. After his hiring, Cooper said he wanted "to try and win a national championship, and, quite frankly, I feel I've got a better chance to do it at Ohio State than Arizona State."

As it turned out, beating Michigan as the ASU head coach turned out to be a lot easier than doing it as the OSU coach. Asked if he thought his record against Michigan and in bowl games was one of the reasons for his dismissal, Cooper said at the time, "I'm sure that was a big factor, and the reason I won't be coaching here anymore.... I had 13 good years here. We won a lot of games. We love Columbus, Ohio.... I will support the next coach at Ohio State."

In 2008 Cooper was elected to the College Football Hall of Fame. He has not been inducted into the Buckeyes Hall of Fame as of this writing.

5

WE LOVE OUR STADIUM

WHAT'S NOT TO LOVE about the greatest college football stadium in the country? Yeah, yeah, Golden Domers, we know all about Notre Dame Stadium. Bottom line is, there would be no Notre Dame Stadium if the University of Michigan didn't graciously come to South Bend a century ago and teach you the game of football.

LSU? Alabama? Wonderful places to watch a game, wonderful traditions…but they're no Michigan Stadium. Texas? Oklahoma? Love the Red River Shootout and the Cotton Bowl—the real Cotton Bowl—but it's no Michigan Stadium.

And as for that school down in Columbus, the armpit of America, well, there's a reason why they call it the Horseshoe. It smells like a stable.

Perhaps the Rose Bowl is the only facility that comes close to rivaling Michigan Stadium, and, really, that's a home away from home for the Wolverines anyway.

No, there's only one Michigan Stadium, and it's located at the corner of Main Street and Stadium Boulevard in Ann Arbor, Michigan.

On game days in Ann Arbor, more than 109,000 pack themselves into The Big House and find out why there really is no place like home.

From six to eight fall Saturdays a year, Michigan Stadium becomes the state of Michigan's fourth-largest city for a few hours when more than 109,000 people pack the place to watch the Wolverines play football. The stadium is a bowl, and three-quarters of it is underground. That was part of the vision of Fielding Yost when he conceived of the stadium, allowing for easier expansion.

Michigan Stadium, though technically part of the university's athletic campus, looks like it was plunked down in the middle of a residential neighborhood. In fact, it was, though the reality is that the 'hood sort of built up around the

stadium, which was built in 1927. Today, traveling north on Main Street leads you into the heart of downtown; south takes you to I-94, the major interstate that leads to both Detroit to the east and to Chicago and points west. But traveling east on Stadium Boulevard takes you past the University of Michigan golf course, Crisler Arena, and into a cluster of houses and apartments; going west on Stadium takes you through a lovely, leafy neighborhood.

According to U-M Bentley Library Archives, in 1893 "the Athletic Field," later known as Regents Field, opened with a capacity of 400. In 1902 Detroit businessman Dexter Ferry donated 21 acres of land to the university just north of the Athletic Field, and the regents changed the name of complex to Ferry Field. Four years later, a new field was built on that land and served the Michigan football team for two decades.

And then Fritz Crisler came along, convincing everyone— especially potential bondholders who were asked to pay $500 each for the construction of a new stadium, a staggering sum in 1926—of the great potential of this sport of football. Crisler worked his magic, Michigan Stadium was built in time for the 1927 season, with 70 rows of seating and a capacity of 82,000, which included the addition of some wooden bleachers.

On October 1, 1927, the Wolverines won their first game at the new facility by defeating Ohio Wesleyan 33–0. Three weeks later, in the dedication game, Michigan beat Ohio State before a then–Michigan Stadium record crowd of 84,401.

From there, here are some notable events in a timeline of the Big House:

1928   Stadium capacity is upped to 85,753.

1930   Michigan becomes the first stadium to erect electronic scoreboards at both ends of the stadium.

1946   Michigan breaks the half-million mark in a season for the first time with 514,598 fans.

1949   Capacity is raised to 97,239 and, in the first year that NCAA attendance records are kept, Michigan leads the nation with an average of 93,894 for each of its six home games. Ohio State averages only 76,429.

1956   Capacity increases again, to 101,001. On October 6 of that year, Michigan Stadium hosts more than 100,000 people for the first time, as 101,001 see the Michigan State game.

1969   On October 4, the Wolverines lose at home to Missouri 40–17. Michigan would not lose another game at home until November 22, 1975, a streak of 41 games.

1973   Capacity is increased again, this time to 101,701.

1975   On November 8, Michigan shuts out Purdue 28–0. The more noteworthy item, however, is that 102,415 fans show up, starting a streak of 100,000-plus attendance that continues to this day.

1996   The Champions Plaza is added and brick pillars and wrought-iron fencing are installed around the stadium perimeter.

1998   An expansion adds another 5,000 seats to increase official capacity to 107,501. But

the new seating area is surrounded by a yellow parapet bearing familiar Michigan icons, including the winged helmet, the university seal, and words from "The Victors." It is universally despised, and fans come to call the monstrosity "the halo."

1999   The Wolverines play their 150th consecutive game in front of at least 100,000 fans with a 37–3 win over Rice on September 11.

2000   "The halo" is removed as then–school president Lee Bollinger acknowledges that "the depth of the criticism and concern seemed to be genuine and coming from reasonable people."

2003   In the season finale, a 35–21 win over Ohio State in the 100th meeting between the two teams, Michigan sets the NCAA single-game attendance mark as 112,118 spectators file through the gates.

2004   In the longest game in Big Ten history, Michigan rallies from 17 down in the fourth quarter to beat Michigan State in triple overtime 45–37.

2006   U-M plays its 200th consecutive game with at least 100,000 fans in attendance in a win over Ball State.

2007   The final portion of the bleacher restoration is completed, and the school announces a new, three-year renovation project of Michigan Stadium that will add premium, luxury seating and a new press box.

2010   The three-year construction project is completed in time for a September 4 rededication of Michigan Stadium.

RIVALRY GAMES

One of the many things that makes Michigan Stadium special is the rivalry games. Obviously, the Ohio State game is one of those, but that's a rivalry that was built out of years of competition, as opposed to, say, logistics or even a feud.

Michigan has two such rivalry, or trophy, games on its schedule. One is obvious—a yearly date with Michigan State, 60 miles up the road in East Lansing. The Wolverines and the Spartans play for the Paul Bunyan Trophy, which was commissioned in 1953 by then–Michigan Governor Mennen Williams. Even though "little brother" has kept the thing for the last three years heading into the 2011 season—an anomaly—the trophy of the mythical woodsman has basically collected most of its dust in the Michigan trophy case. The Wolverines have won 67 and tied five of the 103 matchups with MSU.

But there would be no Paul Bunyan Trophy game—nor any other trophy games for any school, for that matter—if it wasn't for Michigan, the University of Minnesota, an argument over water, and a "little brown jug."

In 1903 Fielding Yost took his famed Point-a-Minute Michigan team to Minnesota with a 29-game winning streak in tow. Minnesota had one of its better teams that year, and the game drew quite of bit of fanfare and attention. When the Wolverines hit the field for the game, however, Yost realized his team

didn't have anything with which to hold water for the players to drink. So he dispatched student-manager Thomas B. Roberts to find something, and Roberts went out and purchased the earthenware brown jug for 30¢.

The Golden Gophers gave Yost's squad all they could handle that day, and when Minnesota scored a touchdown late in the second half that tied the score at 6–6, all hell broke loose. The partisan crowd stormed the field, and officials had difficulty in restoring order. The contest had to be called with two minutes remaining, and the game was declared a tie.

The morning after the game, a Minnesota custodian by the name of Oscar Munson found the jug (although some claim he stole it, which was never proven). Munson brought the jug to Gophers athletics director L.J. Cooke and, according to University of Minnesota archives, said to Cooke in his thick, Scandinavian accent, "Jost left his yug." Cooke decided to keep the jug and painted on its side "Michigan Jug—Captured by Oscar, October 31, 1903," and the score, "Minnesota 6, Michigan 6." The Minnesota "6" was painted far larger than the Michigan "6."

Michigan and Minnesota have been fighting over the Little Brown Jug since 1903. Over the years, the Golden Gophers have worked up quite a thirst. The Wolverines lead the series 66–22–3.

In the meantime, Jost—er, Yost—realized he forgot the jug and wrote to Cooke, asking that it be returned. Cooke replied: "If you want it, you'll have to win it back."

Ironically, the two teams didn't play again until 1909, but Cooke and the Gophers proved to be men of their word— Michigan won the game and took home the jug as the spoils of victory. Ten more years would pass before the two teams played again, with Minnesota taking the prize in 1919. That began a streak of 80 consecutive games, broken only by the Big Ten's unbalanced schedule when the two teams did not meet in 1999 and 2000.

Of course, as far as the series goes, if Minnesota was looking to drink from the jug often, well, it would have died of thirst by now. The Wolverines lead this series 66–22–3.

BOB UFER

You can't love Meeeechigan Stadium without loving the man who broadcast 363 consecutive games from the radio booth in the press box from 1945 to 1981, Bob Ufer.

In the annals of Michigan football, Ufer is as beloved as Yost, Crisler, and Schembechler. His inimitable style, the unabashed, unapologetic love for Michigan that would draw criticism in today's world as being a "homer," the honking of the horn, and all the great "Uferisms" made Bob just as much a part of the program as the winged helmet.

Bob Ufer *was* Michigan—literally. He graduated from the University of Michigan in 1943, having played football as a

freshman but truly excelling in track, setting eight all-time Michigan varsity track records. His time of 48.1 seconds in the 440 at the 1942 Big Ten track meet was the world's best time in the quarter mile and stood for five years—and for 32 years as the Michigan school record.

It was only two years after graduating, in 1945, that Ufer began his radio career. And what a career it was. What got lost in the blatant homerism and off-beat phrases that Ufer used—"Meeeechigan," Bo "General Patton" Schembechler, "cotton-pickin' maize and blue heart"—was the fact that he was a colorful announcer whose folksy manner painted a picture for those listening on the radio.

But it was these Uferisms and calls that made him famous. After the historic upset victory over Ohio State in 1969, Ufer penned, and read on air, this poem:

> *It was November 22, 1969*
> *That they came to bury Michigan,*
> *all dressed in maize and blue.*
> *The words were said, the prayers were read*
> *and everybody cried,*
> *But when they closed the coffin,*
> *there was someone else inside.*
>
> *Oh, they came to bury Michigan,*
> *but Michigan wasn't dead,*
> *And when the game was over it was someone else instead.*
> *Eleven Michigan Wolverines put on the gloves of gray,*
> *And as the organ played "The Victors,"*
> *they laid Woody Hayes away.*

According to a beautifully written piece by author Garry Zonca that appeared in the Ohio State game program a month after Ufer's death in 1981, there were also these beauties:

- In 1969 he described Barry Pierson as, "Going down that mod sod like a penguin with a hot herring in his cummerbund."

- In 1975 he talked about, "That whirling dervish, Gordie Bell, who could run 15 minutes in a phone booth…and he wouldn't even touch the sides."

- In 1976 it was Russell Davis "running through that Buckeye line like a bull with a bee in his ear."

- In 1978 he said, "We're down in the snakepit at Ohio State and our maize in blue dobbers are high right now 'cause we're getting ready to do battle with Dr. Strange-Hayes and his scarlet and gray legions."

- In 1979 Johnny "Wingin'" Wangler and Anthony "the Darter" Carter combined for "the greatest single play in the 100-year history of Michigan football," the touchdown pass with no time left on the clock to beat Indiana.

Early in Schembechler's career as the Michigan coach, Ufer began using a horn in the broadcast booth whenever the Wolverines scored. Ufer said he got the horn from General George S. Patton's nephew, who was willed the horn by the great military man. The nephew was a Michigan fan who listened to Ufer's broadcasts and knew that Ufer compared Schembechler to Patton. The nephew wrote to Ufer, asking

him if he would like the horn that was on Patton's jeep. On the air, Ufer recounted the story and exclaimed, "Would I like it? Is the Pope Catholic?"

The pronunciation of Meeeechigan, Ufer said, was a tribute to the great Fielding Yost. During Ufer's undergraduate days at U-M, while running track indoors, he would find himself wandering over to sit with the old coach—"I can see Yost now with that old felt hat on, chewing on his famous cigar"— and reminisce with the former coach. Yost, Ufer said, had a decidedly southern accent coming from West Virginia and pronounced Michigan as Meeeechigan. "So down through the years on these Michigan football broadcasts, we kind of figured that if Fielding H. Yost could talk about his Meeeechigan, there wasn't anything wrong with old Bob Ufer referring to it that way."

So great was Ufer, so well-known, so well-loved, that he was asked by another Michigan graduate to be the keynote speaker for a rally. The graduate was Gerald R. Ford, who was announcing his kickoff rally for the presidency.

In October 1981, when it became clear that Ufer's days as Michigan's radio broadcaster were drawing to a close due to illness, the Michigan Marching Band spelled out U-F-E-R on the field. He passed away three weeks later.

THE BIG CHILL AT THE BIG HOUSE

Michigan Stadium has been home to countless football games and university graduations. It is rarely, if ever, used for anything else. But on December 11, 2010, the country's greatest

college football stadium turned into the country's greatest outdoor hockey arena for a day.

In an event known as The Big Chill at the Big House, Michigan played Michigan State in a hockey game that drew 113,411 fans—a world record for any outdoor hockey game. It was, in what we can only describe as a simplistic yet superfluous phrase, freakin' awesome!

"I think we all got goose bumps," Michigan forward Carl Hagelin said after a game in which he scored twice in the Wolverines' 5–0 victory. "It was just amazing to see all those people. [It was] probably the loudest environment I've ever been in."

The Big Chill, of course, had a bit of a mixed metaphor. Ostensibly the game was nicknamed that because it was hockey, outdoors, in the middle of December—and it probably didn't hurt that the movie *The Big Chill* centered on several U-M graduates who gather for a friend's funeral. In reality, it was quite comfortable for that time of year, especially in the state of Michigan, with temperatures in the low 40s when the game started. Michigan Stadium was set up with the Olympic-sized rink in the middle of the field, stretching from one 15-yard line to the other. All fans were in seats in the bowl, not on the field, so that fireworks could be set off after goals and for a seven-minute show after the game.

They were wowed. And so were the participants.

"It's definitely one to remember. This is one of the most exciting days of my life," Michigan center Louis Caporusso said. "You get shivers like you can't imagine. It almost brings tears

Movies and TV Shows We Love

AIR FORCE ONE. In the early part of the flick, the president, as played by Harrison Ford, tries to avoid hearing the Michigan–Notre Dame football score so he can sit and watch the game in its entirety during the flight. Damn Russian terrorists.

HOW I GOT INTO COLLEGE. This is an obscure 1980s movie starring a pre-*ER* Anthony Edwards as an admissions officer at fictional Ramsey College. One of the characters is a high school student who wants to go to Ramsey, but whose entire family went to Michigan. There's a scene where the entire extended family is watching a Michigan football game, dressed in maize and blue.

THE BIG CHILL. The classic flick about seven University of Michigan grads who reconvene in South Carolina for a weekend at the funeral of one of their friends, whom they lost touch with since their days in Ann Arbor. U-M is integrated into the movie throughout.

THE PROGRAM. The college football film ends with fictional "ESU" losing to Michigan in a game where Bo Schembechler is featured as a television analyst.

LOST. The popular ABC TV show filled with twists and turns had a unique Michigan connection: the Dharma Initiative was based in Ann Arbor on the U-M campus.

STAR WARS. U-M grad James Earl Jones was the voice of Darth Vader.

NO STRINGS ATTACHED. The 2011 flick starred Ashton Kutcher and Natalie Portman as a pair of love-struck Michigan undergrads.

to your eyes. You can't believe how much passion is at this school. Walking out of that tunnel, hitting that banner, it was something I'll never do again, that's for sure."

"It was a great show. It was a tremendous crowd and a great atmosphere," Michigan State coach Rick Comley said. "Obviously, when you play in something of that magnitude and it comes off that good, they are to be congratulated. The whole thing was great. If you can separate losing, you can't, as a person involved in hockey, experience anything better than what you experienced tonight."

6

WE LOVE OUR CAMPUS
AND CITY

HOW DOES THIS SOUND FOR A LITTLE LUNCH: grilled Amish chicken breast, Wisconsin muenster cheese, spicy fire-roasted New Mexico green chiles, roasted red pepper sauce, lettuce, and tomato on grilled rye bread, followed by a slice of Hunka Burnin' Love Chocolate Cake—four layers of buttermilk chocolate cake covered in rich chocolate buttercream?

That's just a typical sandwich and one of the many desserts you'll find at Zingerman's Delicatessen, arguably the world's greatest deli and marketplace. And found only in Ann Arbor, Michigan.

Ann Arbor is the University of Michigan, and the University of Michigan is Ann Arbor. It's a symbiotic relationship in that the city mirrors the university with an absolutely wonderful, beautiful mix of diversity and ethnicity, with the perfect dash of eclectic spirit thrown in. Ann Arbor is a crazy combination of small-town feel with the culture that rivals a cosmopolitan city. It can be snooty on one day and hippy on the next, but that's what makes it so special.

After all, A2 and U-M have been the home of the Naked Mile and the Hash Bash, two of the more notorious events in the city. The Naked Mile originally was a dash through campus and part of town until both campus and town officials cracked down on the indecency. There hasn't been a Naked Mile—clothed or otherwise—since 2007. Hash Bash still happens on the first Saturday of every April with music, speeches, and a general carnival-like atmosphere advocating the reform of marijuana laws. You might, if you look (and smell) hard enough, find some folks, um, partaking of the theme of the day.

The University of Michigan is split into three campuses in Ann Arbor. Central Campus, where the bulk of the 30,000-plus students go to school, is considered the main campus. We certainly do not need to get into an aesthetics debate between U-M's campus versus Ohio State. Suffice it to say, Michigan's campus is steeped in history and is visually stunning with its Classical and Gothic architecture. Ohio State's campus is also visually stunning, as well—stunning that a "major" university could have the look and feel of a third-rate horror movie.

Central Campus is the original location of the school after the city of Ann Arbor had donated and parceled off 16 acres of land that were originally intended to house the state capitol building. When state lawmakers decided to make Lansing the seat of government in Michigan in a rather foolish and idiotic move, A2 officials instead offered the land to the university, which had been established in 1817 in Detroit. The University of Michigan accepted the offer and moved west to Ann Arbor in 1837; the rest, as they say, is history.

From humble beginnings—Central Campus originally housed one school building, a dorm, and some housing for professors—came the magnificent campus we know today. Central Campus is now the location of virtually every school of study, except for engineering; music, theater, and dance; art and design; and architecture and urban planning. Those studies are on the North Campus. Unlike Central Campus, which is right in the city of Ann Arbor proper, North Campus is a couple of minutes away and detached from the city. The master plan for North Campus and several of its buildings was designed in the 1950s by the outstanding architect Eero Saarinen, who gained fame for designing the Gateway Arch in St. Louis and the TWA Terminal at John F. Kennedy International Airport in New York.

South Campus, of course, is the formal name for U-M's athletic campus. But Central Campus is where it's at. Ten buildings on Central Campus were designed by noted Detroit-based architect Albert Khan, including Hill Auditorium and the totally cool Burton Memorial Tower. The tower, 10 stories high, is actually a clock tower holding one of only 23 grand carillons in the world. The carillon weighs 43 tons and contains 55 bells. The tower is also put to practical use—it houses the university's school of music.

The Michigan Union was where President John F. Kennedy took to the concrete steps outside to announce the formation of the Peace Corps in 1961. Kennedy's successor, Lyndon B. Johnson, returned to U-M in 1965 to announce his Great Society program.

The university also has numerous disciplines and schools of study, including:

MICHIGAN

PLACES WE LOVE

MICHIGAN STADIUM. Do we even need to say anything else about the greatest college football stadium in the country?

THE ROSE BOWL. After all, we've been there 20 times (most in the Big Ten and second only behind USC's 33 appearances). It's a home away from the Big House.

THE DIAG. The coolest place on campus. Everything runs through the Diag, and it's also been the host of everything from outdoor concerts to student demonstrations.

THE ROCK. Located on the corner of Washtenaw Avenue and Hill Street in Ann Arbor, the boulder was first placed there in 1932 as a memorial to honor George Washington on his 200th birthday. When Michigan State fans painted a green "S" on the rock in the 1950s, it obviously needed to be repainted—thus starting a tradition that endures to this day. The Rock has been painted over, for myriad reasons, thousands of times. There's a joke that the Rock is really a pebble and it's just as big as it is now because it's been painted so many times. That's a stretch, but know this—there was a dedication plaque on it, and it was last seen in 1982. Estimates say there's at least a foot of paint covering the Rock.

The **7-ELEVEN** across the street from the stadium in Columbus, Ohio. (You know, just to say hello to all our friends who graduated from OSU and are putting their degrees to good use).

COLLEGE/SCHOOL	YEAR FOUNDED
College of Literature, Science, and the Arts	1841
School of Medicine	1850
College of Engineering	1854
School of Law	1859
School of Dentistry	1875
School of Pharmacy	1876
School of Music, Theatre & Dance	1880
School of Nursing	1893
A. Alfred Taubman College of Architecture & Urban Planning	1906
Horace H. Rackham School of Graduate Studies	1912
Gerald R. Ford School of Public Policy	1914
School of Education	1921
Stephen M. Ross School of Business	1924
School of Natural Resources & Environment	1927
School of Public Health	1941
School of Social Work	1951
School of Information	1969
School of Art & Design	1974
School of Kinesiology	1984

And, what would a great university be without its museums? There are several to choose from at U-M, from the expected to the offbeat. They include the Museum of Art, the Exhibit Museum of Natural History, the Kelsey Museum of Archaeology, Matthaei Botanical Gardens, the Museum of Anthropology, the Museum of Paleontology, the Museum of Zoology, and the Stearns Collection of Musical Instruments, among others.

TALKING THE TALK

If you're going to walk the walk at Michigan, you need to talk the talk. Thanks to the human resource department at the university, here are some "U-Misms" that you need to know.

THE ARB: Nickname for the Nichols Arboretum, a 123-acre "living museum" featuring overlooks and trails through woods and fields, including a stroll along the Huron River.

THE ARCH: The archway through West Hall at the southeast corner of the Diag, also known as the Engineering Arch (from days gone by when the College of Engineering was located on the U-M Central Campus).

BIG BLUES: The name campus bus drivers and many students use to refer to U-M buses that transport students from campus to campus.

THE BREWERY: A historic former brewery on Ann Arbor's north side, now home to several U-M departments.

BURLODGE: The nickname for Bursley residence hall on North Campus.

THE CUBE: Just to the north of the Michigan Union (in Regent's Plaza) is _The Cube_, a sculpture by artist Bernard Rosenthal. It literally is a gigantic cube, balanced—seemingly impossibly—on one point. You can spin it on its axis, although you need to be careful that it doesn't whip around and smack you in the head on the way around.

THE DIAG: The main part of Central Campus. Formerly a pasture, it is now a large area enclosed by campus buildings.

THE DUDE: The James and Anne Duderstadt Center, formerly the Media Union, opened in 1996 as a special place to provide faculty and students with the tools and collaborative space for creating the future. Located on the University of Michigan North Campus, the Duderstadt Center houses the Art, Architecture, and Engineering Library, the College of Engineering Computer Aided Engineering Network (CAEN), the Digital Media Commons, and the Millennium Project. The Mujo Cafe provides a space for refreshment and social interaction. It is named after the former U-M president and his wife.

THE FISH: Ray Fisher Stadium, the home of Wolverines baseball.

THE FISHBOWL: The glassed-in area facing the Diag where Angell, Haven, and Mason Halls meet.

THE GRAD: The Harlan Hatcher Graduate Library.

THE HALF ASS: A cafe/hangout/music and poetry venue located in the lower level of the Residential College, also known as the Half-Way Inn.

THE HILL: A part of Central Campus near the U-M Medical Center that features a cluster of residential dorms, including Couzens Hall, Alice Lloyd Hall, Mary Markley Hall, Mosher-Jordan Hall, Oxford Housing, and Stockwell Hall.

MoJo: The nickname for the Mosher-Jordan residence hall located in the Hill/Observatory area.

The MUG: The ground-floor food court in the Union.

Nat Sci: The Natural Science Building, designed by architect Albert Kahn and completed in 1915, which originally housed the departments of botany, geology, mineralogy, zoology, psychology, and the School of Natural Resources.

The Pringle: Part of the U-M Medical School, the ultra-modern Basic Science Research Building Auditorium (located on Zina Pitcher Place), with its undulating, sloped roof is affectionately known around campus as Pringle Auditorium.

Stepping on the M: The brass M set in the center of the Diag was donated by the university's Class of 1953. Ever since then, students have made a pastime out of not stepping on it. The most common superstition says that if you step on the M, you will fail your first exam at Michigan. Apparently, it's safe to trod on it after that.

The Toaster: This curved-cornered, black-and-stainless steel edifice located on North Campus is home to the UMHS North Campus Administrative Complex.

The U: Shorthand for the University of Michigan.

U-M IN THE OFF-SEASON

Now, when the bulk of students go home in mid-May, it doesn't necessarily mean that the university and town shut

Since 1953 students have avoided stepping on the brass M that is set into the Diag. Stepping foot on it may just cause you to fail your first exam.

down. Far from it. U-M engages in summer classes, like most other schools, and the city of Ann Arbor continues to thrive as the temperature goes up. Two major events happen during the summer. The Summer Festival, which celebrated its 28th anniversary in 2011, is a nearly month-long event from mid-June through early July at U-M's Power Center, Mendelssohn Theater, or Hill Auditorium. Those three venues host nationally and internationally known musicians and entertainers, while the parking garage next to the Power Center features nightly local talent and movies on the top floor, hence known as the "Top of the Park."

In addition, the city of Ann Arbor comes to a virtual standstill for four days in late July for the Ann Arbor Art Fairs, a series of five separate juried art fairs that feature artist and retail booths on virtually every street in the downtown area and up toward Central Campus. Interestingly, though downtown Ann Arbor and the University of Michigan are separated by about a half-dozen blocks between Main Street and South State Street, it's two distinctly different cultures. The State Street area borders U-M's campus and is made up of typical student haunts—bars, clubs, bookstores, budget restaurants, Starbucks, ice cream places, and more. The Main Street area of downtown Ann Arbor is clearly more upscale, with high-end shops and restaurants.

Among these downtown gems is The Earle. Arguably the coolest restaurant in town, The Earle serves French and Italian country cuisine in an elegant setting. The restaurant is literally underground—you enter the building through a set of glass doors and either walk or take an elevator one floor down. It reminds some of an old-fashioned speakeasy from the pro-

hibition era, especially with live jazz five nights a week, but as soon as you walk in the door you'll get a jolt to remind you that this ain't prohibition. There are walls filled with wine corks, and The Earle's wine list is more than 1,000 bottles strong. The restaurant has received *Wine Spectator*'s Best of Award of Excellence for 20 consecutive years. While it's certainly a great spot to bust the budget or take an out-of-towner, The Earle remains a favorite of Ann Arbor locals and certainly one of the most romantic, intimate spots in the city.

Ann Arbor also has one of the most vibrant musical scenes in the country. Since the 1960s, the city has served as a launch pad for such well-known acts as Alice Cooper, Bob Seger and the Silver Bullet Band, George Clinton, and Iggy Pop, among others. One of the best venues in the country for live acoustic music is the intimate setting of The Ark, a non-profit organization that, according to its website, is "dedicated to the enrichment of the human spirit through the presentation, preservation, and encouragement of folk, roots, and ethnic music and related arts. The Ark provides

RESTAURANTS AND BARS WE LOVE

Cubs' A.C., Ann Arbor, Michigan

Scorekeepers, Ann Arbor, Michigan

Fraser's Pub, Ann Arbor, Michigan

Professor Thom's, New York, New York

Tavern on the Tracks, Charlotte, North Carolina

MICHIGAN

a safe and welcoming atmosphere for all people to listen to, learn about, perform, and share music."

The Ark actually began in 1965 as a collaborative effort among four Ann Arbor churches that wanted to host a gathering place for students to hang out. As folk music was prevalent in 1965, it soon became part of the offerings of The Ark, and the rest is history. When the four churches decided in 1977 to no longer support The Ark, the board of directors decided to come up with a fund-raiser for the venue. The nationally known Ann Arbor Folk Festival was born and grew so large that it now uses U-M's Hill Auditorium for such well-known artists as Arlo Guthrie, Ani DiFranco, Roseanne Cash, and many more.

Among the artists who regularly play The Ark is a true Ann Arbor treasure—David Barrett. If you're a true sports fan of any kind, there's no doubt you've heard David's music. He's composed music that plays over television coverage of the Olympics, the U.S. Open (tennis), golf on several networks, and more. But it's been one song that he is most famous for— "One Shining Moment," the tune that is played at the end of the CBS' coverage of the NCAA Men's Basketball Tournament after the championship game, while highlights of the three-week tourney are shown. Ironically, Barrett wrote the song as almost a fluke—he was playing a folk gig and chatting with a worker at the venue and they ended up talking about sports. The woman didn't understand what it was about the essence of sports that made people so passionate. So Barrett went home and wrote "One Shining Moment"— and basically stuck it in a drawer. Then, fortune shined on him.

"In 1985 I was visiting a friend in New York City who just happened to write for *Sports Illustrated* [Armen Keteyian]," Barrett recalled. "We were watching the NBA Finals, talking about sports and life, and I remembered that I had written this song about sports and achievement, so when I got home I sent it to him. He took it over to CBS without me knowing, and they called me up out of the blue."

The 2011 tournament was the 25th year that "One Shining Moment" has been played by CBS at the end of the championship game. In the book *Five Point Play*, which chronicled Duke's 2001 national championship, Blue Devils coach Mike Krzyzewski said, "It's the national anthem of college basketball, and [it's] every kid's dream to appear in that video." The *Wall Street Journal* called it "arguably the most famous song in sports."

> *The ball is tipped*
> *and there you are*
> *you're running for your life*
> *you're a shooting star*
> *And all the years*
> *no one knows*
> *just how hard you worked*
> *but now it shows...*
> *(in) one shining moment, it's all on the line*
> *one shining moment, there frozen in time*
> *But time is short*
> *and the road is long*
> *in the blinking of an eye*
> *ah, that moment's gone*
> *And when it's done*
> *win or lose*

you always did your best
cuz inside you knew...
(that) one shining moment, you reached deep inside
one shining moment, you knew you were alive

Feel the beat of your heart
feel the wind in your face
it's more than a contest
it's more than a race...

And when it's done
win or lose
you always did your best
cuz inside you knew...
(that) one shining moment, you reached for the sky
one shining moment, you knew
one shining moment, you were willing to try
one shining moment.

That led to numerous other opportunities. Barrett recently won a silver medal at the New York Film festival for a hip-hop song in *Don't Cross That Line*, a short film about gambling and student-athletes, and he also won an Emmy for scoring a PBS documentary on writer C.S. Lewis.

"I wish I could say it was career planning, but it's not," he said. "It just worked out that way, and I'm grateful."

And you wonder why we love Ann Arbor so much.

7

WE LOVE OUR FANS

THEY CALL US PRIVILEGED. Arrogant. Stuffy. Overbearing. Unbearable.

And the reaction to that is: Yes. We are. That's what a history of winning does for you. It creates a culture of superiority, and, frankly, why apologize for it? But Michigan fans are also classy, intelligent, knowledgeable, and respectful, the antithesis of the disgusting, foul-mouthed Ohio State fan. Michigan fans are a unique breed; Ohio State fans are inbred.

"We do view ourselves as a different type of fan, and I think that irks the Ohio State fan," says Greg Dooley, who owns and operates the Michigan fan site mvictors.com. "I think it starts with the type of school that Michigan is. You ask the average fan and, yeah, we're smarter. The students are. The fans go way beyond the students, and people back the fact that this is an institution of higher learning. They know how Michigan revolutionized the game. They know the history."

And before you OSU fans start screaming, "We get harassed in Ann Arbor!" No, you don't. The simple fact is Michigan fans don't throw full beer cans at anyone dressed in scarlet and gray, as Buckeyes fans do in Columbus at those dressed

in maize and blue. Going to a Michigan–Ohio State game at the Horseshoe is to set foot in one of the most vile, vulgar, dangerous atmospheres in college football.

But, that's another story. In fact, flip this book over, and we're happy to tell you that story.

In the meantime, this is about a shared passion, a shared allegiance that brings out the best in Michigan fans. Don't know another Michigan fan? Take a walk up Hoover Street on game day and you'll quickly make hundreds of friends. With Michigan, there is a sense of legacy there among the fans.

Troll any Michigan-centric website like mvictors.com, maizeandbrew.com, mgoblog.com, and more, and just take a peek at some of the threads.

"As long ago as I can remember, my parents took me, and eventually, my younger brother and sisters, on an annual trip to Ann Arbor," one poster wrote. "It was where my parents had met, my dad having moved there for work after college, and my mom, three years younger than he, a student at Michigan. I remember, as young as three, spinning the cube on campus or avoiding the 'M' in the Diag. As the years progressed, and the annual fall pilgrimage continued, the memories grew fonder. The dinners at The Cottage Inn, the trips to the MDen, the walks across campus, and of course, football Saturdays. My first trip to The Big House was for the 1995 Michigan–Ohio State game. It was my dad, my grandpa, and me, and we witnessed Tim Biakabutuka run for 313 yards against a formidable Buckeyes defense, leading Michigan to a 31–23 upset win.

If there was any question up until that point as to whether or not I was a Michigan fan, 'Touchdown' Tim removed all doubt from my then-13-year-old mind."

Another wrote: "As a very young kid, before I knew what the game of football was, let alone who Bo Schembechler was, my first stuffed animal was a little yellow bear which I named 'Mazie.' I took the thing everywhere I went."

Dooley said the Michigan–Ohio State rivalry transcends any other football game. "It becomes personal, deeply personal," he said. "People ask me about this all the time, and about the Michigan State game. The rivalry with Ohio State is about who you are, your history, and your history with the school, your family. You find that a little more with Michigan State, but with Ohio State there's a little bit of distance there—yet enough familiarity—to make the rivalry special. Bitter, almost. But there's nothing like it in the world. The moments during pregame, that feeling on the field, is just intense. The Notre Dame game is nice, and Michigan State can be intense, but it's nowhere near the same level. There's so much historical significance on the line with the game."

The rivalry is so emotional, so passionate, that there are few things that unite the two fan bases. When Bo Schembechler died on the eve of the 2006 game between No. 1 Ohio State and No. 2 Michigan, Ohio Stadium went silent in tribute. When the Big Ten hinted that the expansion to 12 teams might cause the Michigan–Ohio State game to be played earlier in the season—or, at least, not as the final game of the year—both sides erupted in anger.

But that's about as far as the camaraderie goes. In early 2011, when OSU showed its true, corrupt self with that Tattoo Scandal (and more on that on the flip side), Michigan fans flocked to buy a T-shirt featuring a humorous image of a coach looking very much like Jim Tressel, wearing his trademark vest but sporting tattoos and a very large gold chain. Above the image is a previous quote from Tressel that reads, "That's what a top-five football team looks like. —Jim Tressel." Under the image it reads: "What happens in Columbus stays in Columbus," with a kicker line under that that says, "Err, unless the NCAA finds out about it!"

Just don't get caught wearing it in the state of Ohio or at an Ohio State bar. Speaking of which, with the biggest alumni base in the country and an active alumni association, you're never alone in your love for Michigan football. You can always find a Michigan fan or two or, you know, dozens, at the following places across the country:

Alaska (Anchorage)—New Peanut Farm

Arkansas (Little Rock)—Beef O'Brady's

Arizona (Gilbert)—Buffalo Wild Wings

Arizona (Scottsdale)—Upper Deck Sports Grill

Arizona (Tucson)—Fox and Hound Pub & Grille

California (Berkeley)—Bobby G's Pizzeria

California (Los Angeles)—Hollywood Billiards

California (Redondo Beach)—Pitcher House Upper Deck

California (San Diego)—Pacific Beach Bar & Grill

California (San Francisco)—Bayside Sports

California (San Francisco)—Blue Light Cafe

California (San Francisco)—The Blarney Stone

California (San Francisco)—Underdog Sports Bar and Grill

California (San Jose)—Double D's Sports Grille

California (Santa Ana)—Tustin Brewing Co.

California (Santa Monica)—South

Canada (Toronto)—Detroit Eatery

Canada (Toronto)—Jack Astor's Bar and Grill

Colorado (Denver)—Lodo's Bar & Grill

Connecticut (New Haven)—Buffalo Wild Wings

Connecticut (Stamford)—Route 22 Restaurant

Florida (Crystal City) Cracker's Bar and Grill

Florida (Key West)—Jack Flats

Florida (Miami)—Upper Deck Ale & Sports Grille

Florida (North Palm Beach)—Duffy's Sports Grill

Florida (Orlando)—Kook's Sports Bar

Florida (Orlando)—Smokey Bones Barbecue

Florida (Tallahassee)—Hobbit American Grill

Florida (Tampa)—Press Box Sports Emporium

Georgia (Atlanta)—Pepperoni's Tavern

Georgia (Atlanta)—Stats

Hawaii (Honolulu)—The Varsity Bar

Illinois (Chicago)—Duffy's Tavern & Grille

Illinois (Chicago)—Mad River Bar & Grille

Illinois (Chicago)—Matilda

Illinois (Chicago)—Moe's Cantina

Illinois (Chicago)—Rockit Bar & Grille (two locations:
    West Hubbard and Wrigleyville)

Indiana (Indianapolis)—Dave & Buster's

Kansas (Kansas City)—Fox & Hound English Pub-Grille

Louisiana (New Orleans)—Cooter Brown's Tavern

Massachusetts (Boston)—The Place

Massachusetts (Boston)—Tavern in the Square

Maryland (Baltimore)—Ropewalk Tavern

Maryland (Bethesda)—Tommy Joe's

Michigan (Ann Arbor)—Scorekeepers
Michigan (Ann Arbor)—The Arena
Michigan (Ann Arbor)—Cub's AC
Michigan (Ann Arbor)—Fraser's Pub
Michigan (Dexter)—Dexter's Pub
Michigan (Glennie)—Glennie Tavern
Michigan (Niles)—Wings Etc.
Michigan (Royal Oak)—Blackfinn
Minnesota (Minneapolis)—508 Bar
Minnesota (Minneapolis)—Majors Sports Café
North Carolina (Charlotte)—Fox and Hound
North Carolina (Charlotte)—Tavern on the Tracks
North Carolina (Raleigh)—Wild Wings
New Jersey (Hoboken)—Black Bear Bar & Grill
New Mexico (Albuquerque)—Fox & Hound Pub & Grille
New Hampshire (Concord)—The Barley House Restaurant
     & Tavern
Nevada (Las Vegas)—Inn Zone Rainbow
Nevada (Las Vegas)—Kopper Keg
New York (New York)—The Ainsworth
New York (New York)—Forum
New York (New York)—Metro 53
New York (New York)—Professor Thom's
New York (Port Chester)—Sam's Bar & Grill
New York (White Plains)—Black Bear Saloon
Ohio (Cincinnati)—Blackfinn Restaurant and Saloon
Ohio (Cleveland)—Fox & Hound Pub & Grille
Ohio (Marysville)—Benny's Pizza
Oklahoma (Oklahoma City)—Iguana Lounge
Oregon (Portland)—Thirsty Lion Pub
Pennsylvania (Philadelphia)—Boat House
Pennsylvania (Philadelphia)—Fox & Hound Pub & Grille

Pennsylvania (Pittsburgh)—Fox & Hound Pub & Grille

South Carolina (Beaufort)—Office Sports Bar & Grill

South Carolina (Charleston)—Mad River Bar & Grille

South Carolina (Columbia)—Bailey's Pub & Grille

South Carolina (Columbia)—Carolina Ale House

South Carolina (Greenville)—Bailey's Pub & Grille

South Carolina (Hilton Head)—Vic's Tavern

Tennessee (Nashville)—Crow's Nest

Texas (Austin)—Pluckers

Texas (Austin)—The Tavern

Texas (Dallas)—Fox & Hound Pub & Grille

Texas (Dallas)—Nick's Sports Grill

Texas (Houston)—Mezzanine Lounge

Texas (Fort Worth)—Fox and Hound

Utah (Salt Lake City)—Green Street Social Club

Virginia (Arlington)—Bailey's Smokehouse & Tavern

Virginia (Newport News)—Bailey's Pub and Grill

Virginia (Richmond)—Bailey's Smokehouse & Tavern

Washington (Seattle)—Buckley's in Belltown

Washington (Seattle)—Rocksport

Washington, D.C.—Buffalo Billiards

Washington, D.C.—Pour House

Vermont (Stowe)—Sunset Grille & Tap Room